Cape
Mediterranean

Ilse van der Merwe

Photography by Tasha Seccombe

Published in 2019 by Struik Lifestyle, an imprint of Penguin Random House South Africa (Pty) Ltd
Company Reg. No. 1953/000441/07
The Estuaries, 4 Oxbow Crescent, Century Avenue, Century City 7441, Cape Town, South Africa
PO Box 1144, Cape Town, 8000, South Africa

www.penguinrandomhouse.co.za

PUBLISHER: Linda de Villiers
MANAGING EDITOR: Cecilia Barfield
DESIGN MANAGER: Beverley Dodd
DESIGNER: Helen Henn
EDITOR AND INDEXER: Joy Clack
PROOFREADER: Linda de Villiers
PHOTOGRAPHER: Tasha Seccombe
FOOD STYLISTS: Tasha Seccombe & Ilse van der Merwe
FOOD PREPARATION: Ilse van der Merwe

Reproduction: Hirt & Carter Cape (Pty) Ltd
Printed and bound in China by C&C Offset Printing Co., Ltd.
ISBN 978-1-43231-022-6

END PAPERS: Design: Beldi, Colour: Deep Jungle – vinyl 'tiled' wall covering by Hertex.

contents

introduction

I've always been fascinated by food and cooking, even as a very young child. It is still like alchemy to me: the magic of creating new flavours and textures by carefully attending to an array of basic ingredients. This fascination became almost an obsession when I discovered the age-old cuisine of the Mediterranean basin (especially Italy, Spain, France, Greece, Morocco, Turkey, Israel and Egypt): the simplicity of their recipes, how they choose only the ripest seasonal ingredients (and do very little to them), their inherent cultural respect across many generations for prolonged meal gatherings and their generous hospitality when entertaining family and friends around lunch and dinner tables.

I grew up in Stellenbosch in the Western Cape, well known for its Mediterranean climate. It is the perfect habitat for vineyards, olive trees and other Mediterranean produce and we have award-winning producers to prove it. Over the past 10–15 years, our way of eating and entertaining in the Cape has evolved away from huge plates of *rys, vleis en aartappels* (rice, meat and potatoes) towards a style that is increasingly similar to classic Mediterranean cuisine: a love of olive oil, nuts, seeds, vegetables and fruit, a love of herbs and spices, eating fresh fish regularly, consuming delicious local wines (well, we've always loved wine) and following an active lifestyle where we make the most of the outdoors in summer. The biggest difference between the South African way of eating and the classic Mediterranean way of eating (especially if you look at the Mediterranean food pyramid) is that we still consume a lot more meat – chicken, lamb, beef and pork – than they do.

In contemporary South Africa, especially in the Western Cape, so many of us love long lunch tables that start with breads and spreads, going into smaller bites or tapas, onto generous salads and vegetable dishes served alongside beautiful roasts or freshly grilled seafood. We savour the process of coming together around a table, many times next to a fire, sharing conversations and creating new memories. We value the hands that bring the ingredients together to nurture our souls and our bodies. We indulge in sweet endings and write thank-you notes to tell each other how much these gatherings mean to us. We spend hours dreaming up new menus for our next get-togethers, choosing local and seasonal ingredients (organic where possible), making friends with our grocers, butchers and speciality shop owners. We know where to find locally produced cheeses, we follow the guidelines for sustainable fish from our vast South African coastlines, and we choose locally produced extra virgin olive oils fresh off the press.

The more well-known Cape Malay, Cape Dutch and indigenous African styles of cooking are well settled within South Africa. With this book, I would like to add another Cape hybrid to our rainbow repertoire: contemporary Cape Mediterranean (#CapeMed) – a South African style of cooking and entertaining influenced by one of the oldest and arguably also the healthiest cuisines in the world.

Join me as I explore our underlying Mediterranean backbone within a thriving, contemporary, multicultural South African foodscape.

Special mention: One of my favourite cookbooks in my home collection is Phillippa Cheifitz's original edition *Lazy Days*. Phillippa is an undisputed South African food icon and has always been an advocate of Mediterranean-influenced recipes and -entertaining. There's no-one who does Cape-Med better and more naturally than her. Thank you, Phillippa, for your endless, effortless inspiration.

What is Cape Mediterranean food/cooking? (#CapeMed)

Cape Mediterranean food/cooking is a contemporary South African hybrid cuisine strongly influenced by the broader Mediterranean basin (Southwestern Europe, Middle East and northern Africa, surrounding the Mediterranean Sea) that has developed naturally from within the Western Cape due to the inherent Mediterranean climate and the abundant occurrence of classic Mediterranean-style local produce. It is not defined by race or ethnicity. Although 'Mediterranean cuisine' is still a term that isn't easily defined and varies across the wider basin, it is mostly accepted to be driven by olive oil, wheat, grapes (wine), fruit, vegetables and seafood, also including dairy and meat.

What are the biggest differences between traditional Mediterranean and Cape Mediterranean?

In South Africa, we traditionally consume more meat than in the Mediterranean basin. Also, our exceptional local olive oil industry is still very young compared to the Mediterranean basin, which has an olive producing history dating back to 2600 BCE, according to some sources. Few of us know how to make fresh homemade pasta or gnocchi (we mostly prefer the quick and easy store-bought dried versions), although they are both very popular items on restaurant menus. However, our culture of alfresco dining because of good weather is shared, as is our love of good wine and an active outdoor lifestyle.

This book focuses on contemporary South African gatherings, not heritage food nor nostalgia. You won't find any twists on milk tart, chakalaka or bobotie. Cape Mediterranean cooking is a natural South African interpretation of classic Mediterranean-style cooking, celebrating our Western Cape-based Mediterranean climate, world-class local produce and dedicated producers.

The Cape Winelands is an incredible place for food lovers and travellers. I was born in Stellenbosch and still live in this historical town with its breathtaking mountains and atmospheric town centre. Coffee culture is an essential part of my daily routine, and there's no better way to stock up on some freshly baked artisanal loaves than from a nearby bakery, such as Boschendal at Oude Bank.

loaves, flatbreads & pizza

basic flatbread

Nothing beats the smell of freshly baked bread from your own oven. It's probably also the nurturing anticipation of breaking open a steamy, delicious, simple piece of bread with friends around a table that makes it so special. Bread may have gained a bad reputation in an era of banting, but if you're not officially allergic or intolerant I urge you to buy a packet of stoneground, unbleached, locally produced flour and try baking your own. It is relatively inexpensive and a highly therapeutic process, and celebrates the unique alchemy of a few very simple ingredients.

Makes 2 large, 4 medium or 8 small

300 g (2 cups) stoneground white bread flour
10 ml (2 teaspoons) instant dry yeast
5 ml (1 teaspoon) sugar
2.5 ml (½ teaspoon) fine salt
200 ml (¾ cup) lukewarm water
15 ml (1 tablespoon) extra virgin olive oil, plus more for oiling the bowl

Mix the flour, yeast, sugar and salt in a large bowl with a spoon. Add the water and oil and mix with a spoon until it starts to clump together, then mix with clean hands to form a dough. Start kneading the dough until it is very smooth – 5–7 minutes (I turn it out onto a clean working surface for better access to kneading space). Shape into a ball and then place in an oiled bowl, cover with a plastic bag and leave to rise in a warm place until doubled in size (about 30 minutes).

Preheat the oven to 230 °C.

Turn out the dough onto a floured surface, then divide into two balls. Roll out each ball into a circular or oval shape, about the size of a large dinner plate (or bigger, depending on your desired thinness). Place the flatbread circle on a large baking tray lined with non-stick baking paper (it's not necessary to dust it with flour), drizzle with some olive oil and sprinkle with salt flakes. Bake for 7–9 minutes or until golden brown and puffy in places.

Serve immediately (break off pieces or slice with a knife).

VARIATIONS

When the flatbread is rolled out and placed on a lined baking tray, you can add the following toppings before baking to create a more exotic flatbread.

Za'atar
5 ml (1 teaspoon) dried origanum
5 ml (1 teaspoon) dried thyme
5 ml (1 teaspoon) ground cumin
10 ml (2 teaspoons) fennel seeds
5 ml (1 teaspoon) ground coriander
5 ml (1 teaspoon) ground sumac
10 ml (2 teaspoons) sesame seeds
5 ml (1 teaspoon) salt flakes
15 ml (1 tablespoon) olive oil

Mix all the dry ingredients together. Use a pastry brush to brush the rolled-out dough with olive oil, then sprinkle generously with the za'atar spice blend and bake until golden.

Onion & rosemary
thinly sliced rounds of red onion (or white onion)
finely chopped fresh rosemary
salt flakes and freshly ground black pepper

Arrange the sliced onions in strands all over, sprinkle with rosemary, season with salt and pepper, then bake until golden.

Garlic & feta
3 cloves garlic, finely grated
15 ml (1 tablespoon) olive oil
1 round feta cheese

Mix the grated garlic with the oil in a small bowl. Use the back of a spoon to spread it onto the rolled-out dough to cover the whole surface, then crumble the feta all over. Bake until golden.

pizza margherita

Once you realise how easy it is to make pizza at home, you may never order in again. Cow's milk *fior di latte* is available in most good supermarkets and it makes all the difference in creating a really milky cheese taste – not rubbery like cheap commercial mozzarellas. Look out for *fior di latte* produced by Zandam and Puglia or get the real deal buffalo version by Buffalo Ridge.

For best results, buy an untreated terracotta tile from your local hardware store (or tile shop) and place it directly on the bottom of the oven before turning on the heat. This way the tile will slowly heat up with the oven (and not crack). The tile also ensures that your oven reaches a temperature that is even higher than its maximum because it radiates heat. Remember to remove the tile only once the oven has cooled.

Makes 2 large or 3 medium

For the base sauce
30 ml (2 tablespoons) olive oil
1–2 cloves garlic, finely grated
1 can (410 g) whole Italian tomatoes, puréed
5 ml (1 teaspoon) sugar
salt and freshly ground black pepper to taste

Heat the oil in a small saucepan over medium heat. Fry the garlic for 15–30 seconds, stirring (don't let it get too dark), then add the puréed tomatoes, sugar, salt and pepper. Stir, then bring to a simmer over low heat. Cook for about 15 minutes until slightly reduced and no longer watery. Set aside.

For assembly
1 batch Basic Flatbread (page 15)
1 batch Base Sauce (see above)
250 g *fior di latte*
a handful fresh basil leaves, to serve

Preheat the oven to 230 °C (use a terracotta tile for best results – see intro paragraph). Roll out the dough into circles as thin as you can – about 30 cm diameter for large pizzas or 23 cm for medium. Place each round on a sheet of baking paper placed on an overturned* baking tray (you don't want to have a lip when you slide the dough into the oven), then use the back of a spoon to spread the base sauce all over. Top with shreds of *fior di latte*, then use the overturned baking tray to carefully slide the pizza with the baking paper onto the heated terracotta tile in your oven. Bake for 7–9 minutes until golden and bubbly. Remove by pulling on a corner of the paper, back onto the tray, and then push the pizza from the baking paper onto a wooden plank. Top with fresh basil, then serve immediately.

* The overturned baking tray and slippery smooth baking paper eliminates the need for a pizza shovel. If you are not using a terracotta tile, replace with a regular solid oven tray or large baking tray that can also be preheated in the same way as the tile. Last option is to just bake the pizza on a cool baking tray as usual (your baking time might be slightly longer).

winelands grape pizza bianca with feta & thyme

The first time I had grapes on a pizza was at my sister's house on Lourensford Farm. They have a brilliant little pizza oven outside, perfect for alfresco feasts. She used red grapes soaked in verjuice, added ricotta, rosemary and a few luxurious pine nuts. Here's my simplified version using white grapes, feta and thyme.

Makes 2 large or 3 medium

1 batch Basic Flatbread (page 15)
±250 ml (1 cup) white grapes, halved
2 rounds feta cheese
2–3 sprigs fresh thyme
salt flakes and freshly ground black pepper

Preheat the oven to 230 °C (use a terracotta tile for best results – see intro paragraph on page 16). Roll out the dough into circles as thin as you can – about 30 cm diameter for large pizzas or 23 cm for medium. Place each round on a sheet of baking paper placed on an overturned* baking tray (you don't want to have a lip when you slide the dough into the oven). Top with grapes, crumbled feta and some thyme leaves, then use the overturned baking tray to carefully slide the pizza with the baking paper onto the heated terracotta tile in your oven. Bake for 7–9 minutes until golden and bubbly. Remove by pulling on a corner of the paper, back onto the tray, and then push the pizza from the baking paper onto a wooden plank. Season with salt and pepper, then serve immediately.

* See page 16.

olive & feta focaccia

This beautiful flat loaf is always a crowd favourite. I use fat, purple, local kalamata-style olives for best results – look out for the incredible kalamata olives from Muiskraal. If you want to go the extra mile, remove the pips before adding the olives (but don't worry, most people won't mind if they're left in).

Serves 6 as a snack

4 x 250 ml (4 cups) white bread flour
10 ml (2 teaspoons) instant dry yeast
7.5 ml (1½ teaspoons) fine salt
375 ml (1½ cups) lukewarm water
10 ml (2 teaspoons) olive oil
125–200 ml (½–¾ cup) preserved kalamata-style olives
1 round feta, cubed

Preheat the oven to 220 °C.

Mix the flour, yeast and salt in a large bowl with a spoon. Add the water and mix until it becomes lumpy. Use your hands to work into a rough ball of dough, kneading for 5–10 minutes to a smooth ball. Oil the ball all over, then place in a bowl covered with a plastic bag to rise in a warm place until doubled in size (about 30 minutes).

Turn out the dough onto a lightly floured surface, then use your hands to pat it out or stretch into an oval shape of about 1 cm thick. Use your fingers to make indentations in the surface all over. Arrange the olives and feta all over, then leave to rise a second time for about 20 minutes. Bake for about 15 minutes or until golden brown. Serve warm, sliced, with extra virgin olive oil, balsamic vinegar and salt flakes.

This is an easy recipe to make by hand, without the need for any fancy stand mixers or equipment.

scott's ciabatta

In 2015/2016, I had the pleasure of working with final year Institute of Culinary Arts (ICA) student Scott Borreros as an intern and my full-time assistant. Apart from being a really nice guy, he was tremendously talented and hard working. Scott showed me this recipe for a great stand mixer ciabatta dough – sticky as hell, but light as air and with a fabulous texture once baked. Once you get the hang of handling the dough you'll agree it is the best ever ciabatta made without a mother starter dough, and in a normal house oven (not wood-fired oven). After his stint at my side, Scott worked at the famous Michelin-star restaurant JAN in Nice, France, for a few years before returning to South Africa in 2018.

Tip: You're going to need a stand mixer and two dough scrapers for this recipe. Buy plastic dough scrapers from a speciality kitchen supply store (like Banks or Value Baking Supplies), or from an online kitchen supply specialist (like Yuppiechef) – they are essential for portioning and handling the sticky dough.

Makes 2 medium loaves or 6 paninis

500 g stoneground white bread flour, plus more for dusting
7.5 ml (1½ teaspoons) instant dry yeast
7.5 ml (1½ teaspoons) fine salt
500 ml (2 cups) lukewarm water

Place the flour, yeast and salt in the bowl of a stand mixer fitted with the paddle attachment (K beater, not dough hook). Mix on low speed. With the mixer running, add the water all at once. Mix for a couple of seconds on low speed to avoid splattering, then turn up the speed to maximum and mix for 8 minutes continuously. Watch the mixer closely, as it tends to 'walk' and might fall off the counter (hold it gently, this is heavy mixing business).

Scrape down the runny dough from the beater using a soft spatula, then cover the bowl with plastic wrap and leave to rise in a warm place until doubled in size (about 45 minutes).

Preheat the oven to 230 °C. Line a large baking tray with baking paper (or use a sieve and dust with flour). Also, dust a large clean working surface with flour, using a sieve.

Remove the plastic wrap and use a soft spatula to turn out the bubbly, runny dough onto the floured surface – do not punch down the dough. Sieve more flour over the top of the dough, then use a dough scraper to cut squares or rectangles out of the dough. Transfer each one as soon as it is cut, using the dough scraper and floured hands, to the baking tray. The dough will feel light as air at this point, almost like marshmallow, but it is very runny and should be handled with lots of dusted flour and a light touch. Leave a little space between the dough portions, as they will rise more in the oven.

Bake for 20–25 minutes until golden brown, depending on the size of your loaves/paninis. Remove from the oven and place on a wire rack.

Serve as sandwiches filled with your choice of filling, or slice up and use as a dipping bread for antipasti platters.

Store leftover bread in plastic bags, and give it a quick refresh in the oven before serving to return it to its full glory. The loaves also freeze very well, covered in plastic.

winelands country-style farm loaf

I'm a huge fan of Ina Paarman's simple, scrumptious recipes. She's one of South Africa's most longstanding food icons, with a history of running her own cooking school, doing fabulous catering and running a very successful family business with her well-known products.

This recipe is based on Ina's 'long-life white bread', especially for the way she rolls up her dough into loaf tins. I've adapted her recipe to use olive oil and to omit the Vitamin C tablet, which she claims will keep the loaf fresh for longer. In my house, the loaf never needs to last longer than one day!

Makes 2 medium loaves

1 kg stoneground white bread flour
1 packet (10 g) instant dry yeast
15 ml (1 tablespoon) fine salt
30 ml (2 tablespoons) sugar
250 ml (1 cup) milk
375 ml (1½ cups) hot water
30 ml (2 tablespoons) olive oil

Mix the dry ingredients thoroughly with your fingers in a large mixing bowl. Combine the milk, water and 15 ml (1 tablespoon) oil, then add it to the dry ingredients and start to mix until it comes together. Continue kneading until you have a smooth, soft, pliable ball of dough – about 10 minutes (turn it out of the bowl and knead on your working surface, dusted with flour if needed).

Use the last 15 ml (1 tablespoon) oil to grease the bowl, then place the dough inside the bowl and cover with a plastic bag. Leave in a warm place to rise until doubled in size (30–45 minutes). In the meantime, spray two medium loaf tins with non-stick cooking spray (or brush with oil).

Punch down the dough, then divide into two. Roll out the dough on a lightly floured surface to a thickness of 2 cm, roll it up into a log shape, then place each roll (seam-side down) in the prepared tins. Leave to rise a second time until they have filled the tins (30–40 minutes). While the dough is rising, preheat the oven to 220 °C.

Bake the loaves for 40–45 minutes until medium-dark brown on top. Carefully turn out of the tins and leave to cool on a wire rack, covered with a clean tea towel. Serve warm or at room temperature, sliced, with butter and preserves.

french-style baguette

Sometimes you just need a long, stylish, thin loaf, like the French's iconic baguette. It's great for making croutons or crostinis and serving with pâté.

Makes 4 large or 6 medium loaves

I use the same dough as the Winelands Country-style Farm Loaf (page 25), but when it comes to shaping the dough after it has risen the first time, I portion it into four (for large baguettes) or six (for medium baguettes) and roll out each one like a sausage. Create a lenthways groove with the pinkyside of your hands, all along the sausage, then fold it in half lengthways on the groove to form a rounded baguette (folded-side down) and thin out the two ends so that they are pointy. Use a sharp knife to score the baguette diagonally, then leave to rise on a lightly floured (or lined) baking tray for 20–30 minutes until doubled in size.

Bake at 220 °C for about 25 minutes or until golden brown. Remove from the oven and leave to cool on wire racks.

See page 24 for photograph.

These make great gifts to take along to a lunch or dinner party. Wrap with unbleached paper and tie with a piece of string.

no-knead cape seed loaf

When serving terrines, I usually serve two types of bread along with them – a white loaf, and a textured seed loaf. My mother used to make the coolest seed loaves in recycled round tins when we were young, and the round slices used to fascinate us as kids.

Makes 1 loaf

750 ml (3 cups) wholewheat flour (nutty wheat)
125 ml (½ cup) bran
250 ml (1 cup) mixed seeds (sunflower, poppy, linseeds, sesame, pumpkin etc.), plus more for sprinkling
10 ml (2 teaspoons) instant dry yeast
7.5 ml (1½ teaspoons) fine salt
10 ml (2 teaspoons) sugar
500 ml (2 cups) warm tap water
15 ml (1 tablespoon) olive oil

Spray a 30 cm narrow loaf tin (or a few clean empty cans) with non-stick spray or oil it thoroughly with canola/olive oil.

Mix the dry ingredients together in a large mixing bowl. Add the water and oil and stir with a wooden spoon until well mixed – it will be a sticky dough. Transfer to the tin using a rubber spatula, then edge the dough into the corners and smooth the top slightly (if using round tins, fill halfway). Cover loosely with plastic and leave to rise in a warm place until almost at the top of the tin (20–40 minutes).

Preheat the oven to 200 °C.

Bake for 50 minutes or until fully cooked and brown. Turn out to cool on a wire rack.

brioche mini-rolls

These little golden rolls may remind you of traditional Cape mosbolletjies, but they're made with regular grape juice and a few pantry staples. Their beautiful round shapes make elegant little dinner rolls served with the best butter you can find. Aniseed has a distinctive liquorice taste. Feel free to substitute* them with fennel seeds, cumin seeds or nigella seeds.

Makes 16

500 g (2⅓ cups) cake flour
5 ml (1 teaspoon) salt
50 g (¼ cup) white sugar
7 g (2 teaspoons) instant dry yeast
15 ml (1 tablespoon) whole *aniseed (not star anise)
60 g (about ¼ cup) butter
125 ml (½ cup) white grape juice
60 ml (¼ cup) lukewarm milk
125 ml (½ cup) lukewarm water
5–10 ml (1–2 teaspoons) vegetable oil, for greasing
30 ml (2 tablespoons) sugar mixed with 30 ml (2 tablespoons) warm water, for brushing after baking

Place the flour, salt, sugar, yeast and aniseed into a large mixing bowl. Stir well with a wire whisk. Heat the butter and grape juice in a saucepan until the butter has melted. Do not boil. Add to the dry ingredients along with the milk and water, then mix by hand until it comes together roughly in a ball.

Turn out the dough onto a lightly floured surface, then knead for 5–10 minutes or until the dough is soft and elastic. Place in a medium-size oiled bowl, then cover and leave to rise in a warm place for about 30 minutes or until doubled in size.

Knock down the dough on a floured surface, then knead lightly for a few seconds. Divide into 16 equal pieces and shape into balls (the correct technique is to squeeze balls of dough through a circle made by your thumb and forefinger, using oiled/buttered hands; this way you get nice smooth balls of dough, tucking in the ends on the bottom). Place the balls on a lined or greased baking tray, then cover with plastic wrap and leave to rise for 30–45 minutes or until doubled in size.

While the rolls are rising, preheat the oven to 180 °C. Mix the sugar and warm water to form a syrup – stir until the sugar is fully dissolved, then set aside. Bake the rolls for 15 minutes or until light golden brown. Remove from the oven and brush immediately with the sugar syrup. Best served warm with butter.

Leftover rolls can be sliced into very thin 'melba toast' slices – dry out in a very low oven at around 100 °C for 20 minutes.

smoky cheese sticks

A roll of buttery puff pastry sometimes saves the day. And these cheesy, golden sticks speckled with smoked paprika are a crowd favourite every single time. Place them in jars on the table or all around the *kuier* area – they're sure to fly as soon as your guests discover them.

Makes about 24

1 roll (400 g) good quality butter puff pastry, thawed
1 egg, whisked
250 ml (1 cup) finely grated Dalewood Huguenot cheese
5–10 ml (1–2 teaspoons) smoked paprika
salt flakes and freshly ground black pepper

Preheat the oven to 220 °C. Line a baking tray with baking paper.

Unroll the puff pastry on a lightly floured surface, then brush with egg all over. Sprinkle the grated cheese all over, season with paprika, salt and pepper, then press down gently to compact the cheese. Cut with a pizza slicer into long sticks. Arrange on the lined baking tray, then bake for 10–15 minutes until golden and puffy. Allow to cool, then serve in jars as a snack.

A strong Cheddar or other hard cheese will also work for this recipe, but Dalewood's award-winning Huguenot has a distinctive nutty, tangy flavour that works so incredibly well here.

roasted garlic butter loaf

Once you've made this loaf, you might never buy a store-bought garlic bread again. This is a fantastic starter to share around a table, served with Loaded Hummus (page 44), or as part of a larger braai spread.

Buying a really good artisanal ciabatta loaf is one of the key aspects to the success of this simple recipe. Your end results will only be as good as the bread you start with.

Don't cut the slices all the way through – this way the garlic butter soaks into the crust on the bottom and doesn't leak out.

Makes 1 loaf

125 g very soft butter
a small bunch fresh flat-leaf parsley, finely chopped (or a mixture of parsley and snipped chives)
1–2 cloves garlic, finely grated
salt and freshly ground black pepper
1 good quality artisanal wood-fired ciabatta loaf

Preheat the oven to 200 °C.

Mix the butter, herbs and garlic together in a small bowl, and then season generously with salt and pepper. Use a sharp bread knife to slice the loaf, not cutting all the way through to the bottom. Spread the slices generously on both sides with the butter mixture (I find that the back of a teaspoon works better than a knife when trying to get in there).

Place on a baking tray, then roast in the oven for 10–12 minutes or until toasted and golden. Alternatively, cover in foil and roast over a fire, turning often, until the butter is fully melted and the bread is golden and toasted.

oil bread

Many years ago, Franck Dangereux released a book while he was still at the helm of La Colombe in Constantia. At the end of that book there are a handful of recipes for breads and rolls, with a quote that says 'bread is the mother of all foods'. I agree, wholeheartedly!

Franck's stunning recipe for 'oil bread' has become a staple in my entertaining repertoire. I once even took a tray of freshly baked oil bread to my daughter's classroom at break time, and the seven-year-old kids devoured it like it was cake.

The only catch is that you do need a stand mixer to make this dough, as it's very wet and sticky and needs to be mixed for 20 minutes (it takes 45–60 minutes by hand, so don't even go there). The end result is a crunchy, salty exterior and a cloudy soft interior with large holes here and there. Magnificent as a starter with hummus or other spreads.

Makes 1 large tray-size bread, enough for 12

1 kg white bread flour
15 ml (1 tablespoon) fine salt
10 g (1 tablespoon or 1 sachet) instant dry yeast
750 ml (3 cups) lukewarm water
45 ml (3 tablespoons) extra virgin olive oil, plus more for drizzling
1 small red onion, finely sliced
2 sprigs fresh rosemary, finely chopped
salt flakes, for topping

Place the flour, salt and yeast in the bowl of a stand mixer fitted with a K-beater. Mix on low speed. Add the water and continue to mix for 20 minutes until the dough is shiny and smooth. On a large baking tray (about 30 x 40 cm, or use two smaller ones), spread out the oil generously with your hands. With your hands still oily, transfer the dough to the oiled tray and leave to rest for 20 minutes. Use your hands again to stretch the dough into the corners of the tray, and your fingertips to poke dimples all over. Cover with slices of onion and chopped rosemary, and sprinkle with salt flakes. Cover lightly with plastic wrap, then leave to rise for about 30 minutes while you preheat the oven to 230 °C. Bake for about 20 minutes until golden brown on top. Remove from the oven and leave to cool slightly on a wire rack, then cut into fingers and serve warm.

dips, spreads & pâtés

chicken liver pâté with brandy, thyme & cream

Chenin blanc is the largest produced grape varietal in South Africa – not because we make so much white wine, but because we make world-class brandy. Cooking with local brandy is very underrated – it adds phenomenal depth to a liver pâté and to many other dishes and sauces.

The secret to making a really great chicken liver pâté lies in adding more than a little butter and a generous amount of salt, and in processing the pâté extra long to create an almost whipped effect, super silky in texture. I also add cream, because it prevents the pâté from hardening too much in the fridge. Don't overcook the livers, they should still be slightly pink in the centre when you process them.

Enough for 6 as a starter

500 g free-range chicken livers
90 g butter, at room temperature
1 onion, finely chopped
1 clove garlic, crushed
2–3 sprigs fresh thyme, woody stems removed, chopped
80 ml (⅓ cup) brandy
60 ml (¼ cup) fresh cream
salt and freshly ground black pepper
bread / melba toast / crackers, to serve

Remove any stringy bits from the livers, rinse them under running water and pat dry.

In a large frying pan, melt half the butter over medium heat. Add the onion and garlic and cook slowly, stirring, until soft and transparent but not brown.

Add the livers and thyme, then fry until the livers change colour – don't let them get too dark. Add the brandy and simmer for 2 minutes over low heat. Remove from the heat when the livers are still pink in the centre.

Place the livers and all the liquids from the pan in a food processor and process until almost smooth. Add the remaining butter and the cream, season generously with salt and pepper (remember the pâté will taste a little less salty when it is cold) and process until very smooth – let the motor run until the pâté is silky, it should take about 2 minutes in an average food processor.

Spoon the pâté into a glass jar or porcelain dish, smoothing the surface. Cover and refrigerate until firm. Serve with toasted bread or crackers.

If you want to keep the pâté from discolouring on the surface (it goes slightly grey after a day), pour clarified butter over the surface, then cover and refrigerate.

smoked cape snoek pâté with apricot jam

When we braai snoek in the Western Cape, it is often basted with a sweet, buttery marinade made with apricot jam. It just works. When I make snoek pâté, it is often with leftover braaied snoek which already contains that little bit of sweetness. The best snoek pâté, however, is made with hot-smoked snoek, which you can buy in most supermarkets almost year round. I add a little apricot jam to match the savouryness of the smoked fish and to mimic the well-loved taste of braaied, basted snoek.

Serves 6 as a snack

about 500 ml (2 cups) flaked smoked snoek (boneless, skinless)
230 g plain cream cheese
15–30 ml (1–2 tablespoons) freshly squeezed lemon juice
a generous handful fresh Italian parsley, finely chopped
10 ml (2 teaspoons) smooth apricot jam (or more, to taste)
salt and freshly ground black pepper

Place the snoek, cream cheese, lemon juice, parsley and jam in a medium-size mixing bowl and mix well (I use a food processor or electric beaters). Taste and season accordingly – sometimes snoek can be quite salty already, so be careful with the salt.

Spoon into a ramekin or pâté bowl and smooth the surface with a spatula. I use kitchen paper to clean and neaten the sides/edges, then cover the bowl with plastic wrap and refrigerate until ready to serve.

This pâté should keep in the fridge as long as the 'best before' date on the smoked snoek packet. If you've made your own smoked snoek using a fresh snoek, the pâté should last at least a week in the fridge.

smoked trout pâté with dill & sour cream

My brother-in-law, Gerhard Compion, farms with rainbow trout on Lourensford Estate in Somerset West. His fish gets distributed countrywide to upmarket supermarkets and restaurants, but it's a treat for us to get really fresh fish straight from him. This easy recipe gets rave reviews every time. Hot-smoked trout keeps fresh in the refrigerator for up to 10 days, so it's a great make-ahead snack for when you're entertaining a crowd or when you're planning a more extensive festive menu. If you prefer a chunky pâté, mix the ingredients with a fork rather than a processor.

Serves 6 as a snack

about 500 ml (2 cups) flaked hot-smoked trout (skinless, boneless)
250 g thick sour cream
30 ml (2 tablespoons) mayonnaise
15 ml (1 tablespoon) freshly squeezed lemon juice
a small handful fresh dill, finely chopped
salt and freshly ground black pepper to taste

Place all the ingredients in a medium-size mixing bowl and mix by hand, using a fork, to the desired consistency – I like mine quite chunky. Taste and adjust seasoning, if necessary. Transfer to a clean ramekin/bowl and refrigerate until needed.

bo-kaap harissa paste

If you haven't been to Atlas Spices in the Bo-Kaap, you need to go. This is the most comprehensive spice shop in the Cape and an institution to visit when in the area. Buy your spices here to make a fiery harissa paste with a collection of the best quality spices in the Cape. It will keep in the fridge for weeks and you can use it in so many creative ways: on chicken, fish and vegetables, in tagines and stews, on breads and as a spicy dip (for a creamy spicy dip, add a tablespoon or two to a tub of cream cheese).

Makes 125 ml (½ cup)

40 g dried smoked red chillies, soaked in 125 ml (½ cup) boiling water for 10 minutes (discard water)
2 cloves garlic, peeled
15 ml (1 tablespoon) ground coriander
15 ml (1 tablespoon) ground cumin
15 ml (1 tablespoon) fennel seeds
2.5 ml (½ teaspoon) salt
60 ml (¼ cup) olive oil, plus extra

In a small food processor bowl, pulse all the ingredients together to get a chunky paste. Place in a glass jar, cover with a thin layer of olive oil, then cover and refrigerate until needed. Will keep for at least two weeks in the fridge.

Use this harissa paste to make a delicious Mussel & Tomato Stew (page 86) or a Chicken, Chickpea & Couscous Soup with Cumin & Fresh Mint (page 95).

loaded hummus

I am a huge fan of Yotam Ottolenghi, the famous British-Israeli restaurateur and food writer. His recipe for hummus in his award-winning cookbook *Jerusalem* changed the way I eat and serve hummus: he processes his hummus until it is super-smooth and creamy, then tops it with chopped olives, parsley, roasted pine nuts and olive oil. It is simply dreamy – this simple yet opulent dip, spread out wide on a shallow dish.

Making hummus from raw chickpeas is, in my opinion, far superior to using canned chickpeas. Once you've seen and tasted the results, you'll agree that it is truly worth the extra time it takes to make.

Served with fresh, crusty bread, it's all you need for a simple meal but it also makes a fabulous informal starter.

Note: This recipe requires a few hours of soaking, so start the previous day if you want to make it for lunch.

Serves a crowd

250 g uncooked organic chickpeas
10 ml (2 teaspoons) bicarbonate of soda
125 ml (½ cup) freshly squeezed lemon juice
30 ml (2 tablespoons) extra virgin olive oil, plus extra for drizzling
1 clove garlic, finely grated
80 ml (⅓ cup) tahini (sesame paste)
1 ml (¼ teaspoon) ground cumin
salt
60–125 ml (¼–½ cup) cold water
125 ml (½ cup) kalamata olives, pitted and chopped
a generous handful fresh Italian parsley, finely chopped
30 ml (2 tablespoons) pine nuts, roasted in a dry pan

Place the chickpeas and 5 ml (1 teaspoon) bicarbonate of soda in a ceramic bowl and cover with water to a level of about 5 cm above the chickpeas. Soak for at least 3 hours, but preferably overnight. Drain and rinse the chickpeas, then transfer to a medium-size pot. Add the remaining 5 ml (1 teaspoon) bicarbonate of soda and cover with fresh water to the same level as before. Bring to a boil, then simmer until tender and almost falling apart, skimming off any foam from the surface.

Transfer the cooked chickpeas to a food processor (or better yet, a power blender) along with the lemon juice, olive oil, garlic, tahini, cumin and some salt. Process to a fine, creamy purée, adding enough cold water to loosen it up and get a really smooth result – the magic is all in the texture. Taste and adjust the seasoning, if necessary. Store in the fridge until ready to serve – it needs some time to rest and for the flavours to develop, so it's best to make ahead.

Serve at room temperature (give it a good stir before plating) on a shallow wide plate, topped with chopped olives, parsley and roasted pine nuts with a generous drizzle of olive oil and some crusty bread on the side.

The hummus will keep well in the fridge for at least four days.

double-cream tzatziki

After travelling to Greece in 2010, I was mesmerised by the texture of real Greek tzatziki. Their yoghurt is almost as thick as cream cheese – nothing watery about it at all – and is luxurious, thick and spreadable, full flavoured and well seasoned. We rarely get triple-strained yoghurt in South Africa, but Fairview does deliver with their small tubs of full-fat strained yoghurt. It makes the closest tzatziki to a proper Greek one, so take the time to find it and you'll be amazed by the results. Of course, properly drained cucumber also adds to the result, so follow my method below and you'll have a winning dip.

Makes about 750 ml (3 cups) or enough for 6–8 people

½ English cucumber
500 ml (2 cups) double-cream yoghurt
1 clove garlic, finely grated
a small bunch fresh mint leaves, finely chopped
salt and freshly ground black pepper to taste
15 ml (1 tablespoon) extra virgin olive oil

Halve the cucumber lengthwise, then scoop out the seeds using a teaspoon. Place a clean, folded tea-towel on your work surface, then grate the cucumber coarsely over the towel. Cover the cucumber with the towel, then wring it firmly to get rid of all the juices. Unroll the wringed cucumber and place it in a mixing bowl, scooping all the little bits from the towel into the bowl. Add the rest of the ingredients, then mix well. Taste and adjust the seasoning, if necessary, then cover and refrigerate until ready to serve.

basil pesto

Just outside Stellenbosch, off the R44 on the Raithby Road, my friends John and Jolene House run an organic farm producing small batches of vegetables, herbs and foraged duck eggs. Their basil and tomatoes are legendary. Use the basil stalks-and-all for pesto – the flavour of the stalks (discard any woody ones) is the same as the leaves. When my budget doesn't allow for the more traditional pine nuts in this pesto, I use a handful of cashews or almonds – they make a fantastic substitute.

Makes 125 ml (½ cup)

40 g (2 small punnets) fresh basil
1 clove garlic, peeled
30 ml (2 tablespoons) pine nuts, lightly roasted in a dry pan
60 ml (¼ cup) finely grated Parmesan cheese
80–125 ml (⅓–½ cup) extra virgin olive oil
salt and freshly ground black pepper to taste

In a food processor or electric chopper (or manual pestle and mortar), process/pound all the ingredients together to make a chunky paste. If using a pestle and mortar, chop the ingredients by hand first. You're looking for a chunky paste, not too runny, but not too dry. Taste and adjust the seasoning, if necessary. Use immediately or transfer to a jar, cover with a thin layer of olive oil, cover and refrigerate until ready to use.

Fresh basil will discolour after a few hours. If not using the pesto immediately, blanch the basil in simmering water for 5 seconds. Transfer to iced water, then drain. Continue the recipe as above. The pesto will keep for four days, covered and refrigerated.

olive tapenade with anchovy & capers

There's a farm on the Helshoogte Pass that produces some of my favourite local extra virgin olive oil and lovely, plump olives. Tokara is also well-known for their immaculate fine-dining restaurant and more relaxed deli. Their olives and oils are based on the age-old Italian methods of cold pressing – you can even taste some in their deli.

Make your own spectacular, punchy olive tapenade by blending your favourite olives with a few anchovies and capers. It's a grown-up festival of astringency!

Makes about 250 ml (1 cup)

500 ml (2 cups) preserved kalamata olives, pitted
2–3 small anchovy fillets in oil, drained
15 ml (1 tablespoon) preserved capers, drained
juice of ½ medium lemon (10–15 ml/2–3 teaspoons)
30–60 ml (2–4 tablespoons) extra virgin olive oil

Place all the ingredients in a blender and pulse to a medium smooth paste, adding just enough olive oil to get a spreadable consistency. Transfer to a jar or bowl, cover and refrigerate until ready to use. Will keep in the fridge for at least two weeks.

It can be time-consuming to pit olives. A proper olive pitter seems to be quite costly these days, so if you don't have one, phone a friend to help with the labour and pour a glass of wine at once.

almond dukkah

Dukkah is a phenomenal addition to a tapas-style spread that already includes fresh bread and extra virgin olive oil. It is really easy to make and tastes so much more fragrant when freshly made compared to store-bought versions.

I like making my dukkah with whole almonds, because they result in a darker mixture because of the skins, with superb crunch when freshly roasted.

Makes about 250 ml (1 cup)

250 ml (1 cup) whole almonds
60 ml (¼ cup) sesame seeds
10 ml (2 teaspoons) ground cumin
5 ml (1 teaspoon) ground coriander
2.5 ml (½ teaspoon) sumac or smoked paprika
10 ml (2 teaspoons) salt flakes
bread and extra virgin olive oil, to serve

Preheat the oven to 180 °C.

Spread the almonds out on a baking tray, then roast for 8–10 minutes until toasty. Place the almonds in a food processor or chopper and process for a few seconds until most of the nuts are finely chopped with some coarser chunks remaining – don't process too long or you'll make almond butter. Transfer to a mixing bowl.

In the meantime, place the sesame seeds in a pan and toast over medium-high heat on the stovetop until golden, stirring often – be careful, they burn easily. Add to the chopped almonds, then add the cumin, coriander, sumac/paprika and salt flakes. Mix thoroughly with a spoon. Serve with bread and extra virgin olive oil, for dipping.

Store in an airtight container and use within 2–3 weeks.

CHAPTER 3:

tapas, terrines & tasters

pan-fried calamari tentacles with chorizo, olive oil, lemon & herbs

We were once invited to join a friend for sundowner drinks at his amazing luxury 'tent house' at Keurboomstrand, where he lives permanently with his pointer dog. On a whim, I made a tapas-style calamari dish in his kitchen that day that has since become a staple in our family. The flavour of this dish is quite dependent on the quality of the chorizo, so buy the best you can afford and you're pretty much there already.

Serves 6 as a snack

30 ml (2 tablespoons) extra virgin olive oil (plus 45 ml/3 tablespoons more for drizzling at the end)
200 g good quality chorizo, skin removed, sliced into thin half circles
500 g frozen baby calamari tentacles, cleaned and thawed
5–10 ml (1–2 teaspoons) smoked paprika
5 ml (1 teaspoon) dried chilli flakes (optional)
juice of 1 lemon (or more)
a large handful fresh parsley and/or coriander, roughly chopped
salt and freshly ground black pepper to taste
a loaf of fresh rustic bread, to serve

Heat a large heavy-based pan or iron skillet until very hot. Add the oil and fry the chorizo, stirring quickly until it starts to brown. Add the calamari, paprika and chilli flakes and fry over high heat, stirring, for 1–2 minutes until just cooked. Remove from the heat, add the lemon juice, more olive oil and parsley and/or coriander. Stir, making sure you loosen any sticky bits on the bottom of the pan, if any. Test for seasoning, then add salt and pepper to taste. You're looking for a result that is not soupy, but instead 'wet' with punchy, red, herbacious, lemony oil and liquid around the calamari to enjoy with your bread.

If your pan is not hot enough, the calamari will release a lot of moisture and it will just simmer instead of fry. If this is the case, drain some of the liquid and continue over very high heat to reduce it before adding the lemon juice, etc. Be careful, though, not to overcook the calamari while trying to reduce the liquid – it can become rubbery.

roasted rosa tomatoes with garlic & thyme

If you have a punnet of baby tomatoes in your pantry (especially if they are not the perfect tomatoes to enjoy as is), roasting them will not only make your kitchen smell like a Mediterranean getaway, but it will also turn any simple meal into a feast. Serve them as a side dish, as a topping for crostinis with labneh or *fior di latte*, in a salad, tossed with pasta, with a cheese board or just on their own.

Serves 6

500 g rosa tomatoes (or cherry/baby tomatoes)
3 cloves garlic, peeled and thinly sliced
45–60 ml (3–4 tablespoons) extra virgin olive oil
15–20 ml (3–4 teaspoons) red wine vinegar
15 ml (1 tablespoon) brown sugar
3–4 sprigs fresh thyme, woody stalks removed
salt and freshly ground black pepper

Preheat the oven to 160° C.

On a standard baking tray (23 x 35 cm), spread out the tomatoes and garlic slices in a single layer (for larger tomatoes, halve them but keep small ones whole and keep vine tomatoes on the vine). Drizzle with oil and vinegar, then season all over with brown sugar, thyme, salt and pepper. Roast for 1–1¼ hours, or until the edges turn dark and sticky. Remove from the oven. Serve hot or at room temperature.

For an even better treat, bake these tomatoes on a larger baking tray with added slices of onion and whole rounds of feta. This makes a fabulous side dish for your next braai.

grilled marinated sweet peppers with garlic & olive oil

To me, alfresco foods like grilled vegetables on bruschetta make for the perfect snacks all year round. And with the intensely bright red, orange and yellow hues that come with grilling really fresh peppers, it's like a piece of sunshine on a plate.

You can certainly serve these peppers warm on a very cold day, but I mostly prefer eating my marinated peppers at room temperature. Freshly toasted warm bruschetta is obligatory though, as it really soaks up the lovely sharp marinade.

Serves 6–8 as a snack/starter

4 large red/orange/yellow peppers (or 6 medium)
olive oil for greasing
about 80 ml (⅓ cup) extra virgin olive oil
30–45 ml (2–3 tablespoons) apple cider vinegar
salt and freshly ground black pepper
slices of baguette (or sour dough or ciabatta), soft goat's milk cheese and fresh basil leaves, to serve

Preheat the oven to 230 °C.

Remove the seeds and pith of the peppers, then slice into large flat 'panels'. Grease a baking tray with olive oil, then arrange the peppers skin-side up. Roast the peppers for about 25 minutes, or until the skin starts to blister and turn black. (Note: If you have access to an open fire at a braai, place the peppers on an open grid and turn them every few minutes with tongs, until they are black and blistered all over.)

Remove the peppers from the oven, then place them immediately (with all the juices from the pan) in a plastic container that can seal tightly. Close the lid and leave to steam and cool for at least 15 minutes.

Now remove the skins from the peppers – they should peel off easily. Discard the skins. (Note: If you grilled whole peppers over a fire, now's the time to remove the pith, seeds and skin.)

Cut the soft fleshy peppers into strips 5–10 mm wide, then place them back into the plastic container. Add the olive oil and vinegar, and season well with salt and pepper. Mix with a spoon, taking care not to break up the peppers.

Leave to marinate for a few hours – the flavours will improve with time. Refrigerate until ready to use, then return to room temperature before serving.

Serve on slices of freshly toasted bruschetta, topped with goat's milk cheese, peppers and some fresh basil leaves.

grilled marinated aubergine with garlic, lemon & mint

I absolutely adore aubergines and will eat them any way possible, but this is definitely one of my favourite ways of serving them. I've converted quite a few aubergine haters to aubergine lovers over the years with this recipe!

The secret lies in cutting them super thinly – you really need a mandolin cutter for this. Then you grill them without any oil in a super-hot griddle pan until they are charred. Finally, the warm slices get drenched in a punchy marinade made from extra virgin olive oil, freshly squeezed lemon juice, crushed garlic, fresh and dried mint, some salt flakes and freshly ground black pepper. They soak up a lot of the marinade, and are simply exquisite served at room temperature on crusty toasted bruschetta. The flavour of the olive oil really shines through, so use your favourite, grassy varietal (like frantoio).

Note: The batch grilling might seem tedious, but I promise you it's really worthwhile. You can also try doing it on an open grid over a medium-hot fire – extra smoky flavours for the win. Also, it's amazing how far two aubergines are stretched with this recipe.

Serves 6

200 ml (¾ cup) extra virgin olive oil
juice of 1 lemon
2 cloves garlic, finely grated
5 ml (1 teaspoon) dried mint (optional)
a handful fresh mint, finely chopped
salt flakes and freshly ground black pepper to taste
2 large aubergines, thinly sliced
sliced bruschetta, toasted, to serve

Combine the olive oil, lemon juice, garlic and dried and fresh mint. Season generously with salt and pepper.

Heat a griddle pan over high heat on the stovetop. Fry the slices of aubergine in batches until lightly charred and softened. Remove each batch from the grill and layer them in a glass/ceramic plate or baking dish, drizzling each layer generously with marinade. If there is any marinade left, spoon it all over the top layer.

Cover the plate and leave to cool to room temperature. Serve on toasted bruschetta.

This dish, covered, keeps well in the refrigerator for a few days. Return to room temperature before serving.

The grilled marinated aubergine will darken slightly after a day or two – don't be alarmed.

roasted garlic prawns
with lemon & herbs

At the time of writing this book, prawns were orange listed on SASSI's sustainability list. However, you can still find sustainably farmed prawns in many supermarkets – be sure to look for the marking on the outside of the packet. Prawns are such a hit for entertaining and they are incredibly easy to cook. This is a recipe that needs some crusty bread to mop up the lovely oily sauce.

Serves 6 as a snack

about 800 g sustainably farmed prawns, thawed and rinsed if frozen
4–6 cloves garlic, peeled
1 small chilli, sliced (optional)
finely grated rind and juice of 1 lemon, plus 3 more for serving as wedges
80 ml (⅓ cup) extra virgin olive oil
a handful fresh parsley and/or coriander
salt and freshly ground black pepper
crusty bread, for serving (optional)

Preheat the oven to 230 °C.

Clean the prawns by cutting the shells open from the necks to the tails and lifting out the digestive tracts. Place the prawns in a large, deep roasting tray. Place the garlic, chilli, lemon rind and juice, olive oil and herbs in a small blender or food processor. Season generously with salt and pepper, then process to a pulp. Pour the pulp over the prawns and stir with a spatula until the prawns are coated in the mixture. Spread out the prawns in a single layer. Roast for 7 minutes, then use the spatula to stir and turn the prawns over. Roast for another 7 minutes. Serve hot with crusty bread and fresh lemon wedges.

Roasting these prawns whole (head on, shell on) creates much more flavour than just using the cleaned tail meat. Most of the flavour of prawns comes from the heads. Save the roasted heads and skins for use in a deeply flavoured seafood stock for your next Cape Seafood Stew (page 89).

grilled asparagus
with hollandaise sauce

Classic French hollandaise sauce works so well with grilled asparagus, especially if you use fresh lemon juice instead of vinegar. You can serve these as a side dish, as a starter, as part of a brunch buffet, or even as a salad on a bed of rocket. Don't be scared of making hollandaise – once you get it right, you'll never look back. Cooking something over a pot of simmering water (double boiler) is not as technical as it seems – you only need a little elbow grease and good timing.

Note: For an extra touch of luxury or for a special occasion, wrap each spear in thinly sliced prosciutto before pan-frying for a minute or two, then drizzle with the hollandaise and top with toasted flaked almonds.

Serves 4 as a starter or a side dish

Hollandaise sauce
3 extra-large egg yolks
30 ml (2 tablespoons) lemon juice
125 g cold butter, cubed
salt and freshly ground black pepper to taste

Asparagus
15–30 ml (1–2 tablespoons) extra virgin olive oil
16–24 asparagus spears (not too thin)
30 ml (2 tablespoons) flaked almonds, roasted in a dry pan
a handful micro herbs, to serve (optional)

For the hollandaise, place a small pot filled with 5 cm water on the stove and heat to a slow simmer (not a rolling boil). In a slightly wider heatproof bowl (glass or stainless steel), add the yolks and lemon juice. Place the bowl over the simmering water, taking care that the bottom of the bowl doesn't touch the simmering water. Start whisking the egg mixture immediately, whisking steadily as it heats up. When the mixture warms up and starts to thicken (after 3–5 minutes), add a few blocks of butter and keep on whisking as it melts into the mixture. Keep on adding more butter until all the butter is melted and incorporated, and you are left with a thickened, savoury custard-like sauce. Season with salt and pepper.

NB: If, at any stage, your mixture becomes too thick or looks like it wants to split, remove it from the heat and add more cold butter to bring the temperature down, then continue as above.

Remove the sauce from the heat when done and set aside until ready to use. (Add a teaspoon or two of boiling water to the mixture to bring it back to pouring consistency just before serving, if necessary.)

For the asparagus, heat the olive oil in a wide pan or skillet, then fry the spears for just a few minutes until they get some golden colour. Don't let the spears start to wilt – rather undercook than overcook them. Transfer to a serving platter, drizzle with hollandaise, and scatter with roasted almonds and micro herbs. Serve at once.

steamed saldanha bay mussels in sauvignon blanc & herbs

When you have access to a bunch of really fresh mussels straight from the West Coast, do as little to them as possible – savour their delicate texture by steaming them in some great local dry white wine and a few aromatics just for a few minutes until they open. No stodgy flour-based sauces that kill the freshness of the ocean. Just a light, brothy, salty liquid with fresh herbs that makes the most of the incredible mussels.

These days you can order pristine farmed mussels (sustainably rope-grown) directly from Blue Ocean Mussels in Saldanha, delivered to your door. Check them out online: blueoceanmussels.com

Serves 6 as a light meal or starter

2 kg fresh live black mussels
15 ml (1 tablespoon) extra virgin olive oil (or butter)
about 250 ml (1 cup) finely sliced leeks, white part only (or white/red onions, finely chopped)
2 cloves garlic, finely chopped
375 ml (1½ cups) dry white wine
a large handful (about 20 g) fresh Italian parsley, roughly chopped
fresh, crusty bread, to serve

Rinse the mussels under cold water. Discard any mussels with broken shells. Scrub any barnacles from the shells using a small knife (preferably not your best knife) or hard scrubbing brush. Remove the beards by pulling them from the pointy edge of the shells towards the round edge (not all mussels will have beards). Rinse once again and drain in a colander.

Heat the oil in a large, wide pot and fry the leeks until just soft. Add the garlic and fry, stirring for 30 seconds. Add the wine and bring to a simmer. Add the mussels and cover with a lid. Bring back to a simmer and cook for 5–8 minutes, steaming the mussels until they are open* (don't overcook them at this stage). Remove from the heat and sprinkle half the parsley over the mussels, giving them a quick stir. Serve at once, with more parsley, in bowls. Enjoy with crusty bread to dip into the broth.

Note: Store fresh live mussels in a bowl in the fridge, with some room to breathe (not in a closed container). Drain any excess sea water (that forms in the bottom) daily and rinse before use.

* For safety, discard any mussels that aren't open after cooking.

smoked paprika & rosemary roasted nuts

Snacking on a bowl of roasted salty nuts makes me feel very pampered. Considering the price these days, it's a luxury item that I reserve for special occasions. However, if you should come across a great deal on buying nuts in bulk, do try this easy recipe. Served warm, it's a fabulous way of making guests feel looked after while serving the first round of drinks at your dinner party.

If your budget is tight, opt for a bag of giant skinless peanuts – they also work beautifully with this recipe.

Interesting fact: South Africa is the biggest producer of macadamia nuts in the world. They are mainly grown in Limpopo.

Makes 2 cups, enough as a snack for 6–8 people

200 g mixed raw nuts (macadamia, cashew, pecan, brazil, walnut, large peanut, etc.)
10 ml (2 teaspoons) extra virgin olive oil
10 ml (2 teaspoons) honey
10 ml (2 teaspoons) smoked paprika
10 ml (2 teaspoons) salt flakes
5–10 ml (1–2 teaspoons) finely chopped fresh rosemary

Preheat the oven to 180 °C.

Combine all the ingredients in a medium-size mixing bowl, stirring until all the nuts are well coated. Spread the nuts out on a baking tray in a single layer. Roast for 15 minutes, then remove from the oven and stir with a spatula. Spread out again evenly, then roast for another 7–10 minutes until golden brown and fragrant. Remove from the oven and leave to cool for a few minutes before serving. Serve hot or at room temperature. (If not serving immediately, leave to cool to room temperature, then store in an airtight container.)

baked winelands brie with nuts & honey

This is not technically a recipe, it's more of a serving suggestion. There are so many incredible soft cheeses available in South Africa, so choose whichever is your favourite. For most people, there's something totally addictive about a melted chunk of cheese – it's the weirdest thing to see when your guests delve into this baked Brie and it just starts oozing the most delicious milky goo. People just go crazy for it. Also, you wouldn't necessarily ever serve a Brie just on its own, but in its baked form it becomes a stunning dish in its own right. It's a winner – try it.

Serves 4

1 Brie cheese (125 g)
15–30 ml (1–2 tablespoons) nuts (pecans, macadamias, almonds, cashews or a mix), roughly chopped
15–30 ml (1–2 tablespoons) honey, for drizzling
sliced baguette, to serve

Preheat the oven to 180 °C. Place the Brie on an ovenproof small plate, then top with the nuts. Bake for 8 minutes, then remove and drizzle with honey. Serve at once, with sliced baguette for dipping.

country-style pork & port terrine with pistachios

This terrine is based on the classic French *terrine de campagne*, or country terrine. It's a grown-up dish, and something that reminds me of my grandmother, Naomi Uys. She was the one who introduced me to exotic meats like beef tongue, turkey and stuffed venison back in the 1980s. She used to make and serve the most incredible cold meat spread at Christmas time at their camping spot at Buffels Bay (yes, from her camping kitchen!). It also included pickles and mustard – something I only learned to love as an adult. Once you discover these 'grown-up' delicacies, you can't go back.

A meat terrine is not difficult to make, but it takes a little effort and some time. Make it a day ahead of your festive occasion, as the loaf needs time to set in the fridge and the flavours really develop over time. I use a local port (something from Calitzdorp would be fantastic) but you can also use a combination of red wine and brandy to add depth of flavour. The pistachios look amazing when you slice the terrine – the green specks scattered like little treasures – and they provide a welcome crunch.

Be sure to serve this terrine with lots of different pickles and/or sweet jellies – gherkins, pickled onions, wholegrain mustard and Port-soaked Cranberries (page 189). Add a loaf of your favourite bread and a glass of fortified wine, and this becomes a feast of epic proportions.

Serves 10–12

15 ml (1 tablespoon) butter
15 ml (1 tablespoon) extra virgin olive oil
1 onion, finely chopped
3 cloves garlic, finely chopped
3 sprigs fresh thyme, leaves only
6 fresh sage leaves, finely chopped
250 g smoked streaky bacon
about 800 g rindless pork meat with some fat, cut into smaller chunks (loin/shoulder/neck/rashers)
250 g fresh chicken livers
250 ml (1 cup) port
5 ml (1 teaspoon) grated nutmeg
2.5 ml (½ teaspoon) ground allspice
5 ml (1 teaspoon) fine salt
2.5 ml (½ teaspoon) ground black pepper
100 g pistachio nuts, shelled
bread, pickles and preserves, to serve

Preheat the oven to 180 °C.

Heat the butter and oil in a large pan over medium heat, then add the onion, garlic, thyme and sage and fry until the onion is soft and translucent but not brown. Remove from the heat and set aside to cool.

Line a 30 x 11 x 7 cm loaf tin with non-stick baking paper, leaving some of the paper hanging over the sides (it needs to be folded over the top later). Arrange the streaky bacon inside the loaf tin, packing the strips tightly together over the width of the tin, not overlapping. There should be a few pieces left – save them for arranging over the top at the end.

Place the cooled fried onions, pork, chicken livers, port, nutmeg, allspice, salt and pepper in a food processor, then process until you get a coarse paste resembling minced meat. Transfer the paste to a mixing bowl, then stir in the pistachios.

Continued on following page

Continued from previous page

Spoon the mixture into the loaf tin and smooth the top with a spatula. Top with the last few pieces of bacon, then fold the hanging pieces of baking paper over the top to seal the terrine. Use extra paper if necessary. Now cover the top tightly with foil. Place the loaf tin in a larger roasting tray, then fill the roasting tray with hot water (hot tap water is fine). The water level should come up to 2–3 cm from the top.

Bake the terrine for 2 hours. Remove the terrine from the oven, then carefully remove the loaf tin from the roasting tray. Place the tin on a wire rack for another 30 minutes without removing the foil or wrap.

Now weight the terrine (this is an important step, as it will make the terrine more compact and easier to slice when cooled): Cut a piece of cardboard the same size as the inside of the top of the tin, then place it on top of the terrine with a few heavy objects on top (I used three cans of food). When the terrine is completely cool, place it in the refrigerator for at least 4 hours or preferably overnight (with the weights on top). There should be some liquid in the tin – don't worry, it will jellify in the fridge and most will get absorbed into the terrine.

When ready to serve, open up the top layers of baking paper and turn the terrine out onto a board or serving tray. Carefully remove the paper. Serve sliced, with your choice of pickles and jellies or port-soaked cranberries.

The terrine will keep well in the fridge for at least a week in an airtight container. It gets more delicious over time.

free-range duck liver terrine/parfait

To clarify, this is not foie gras or any type of questionable duck dish. This is a natural duck liver terrine, made with free-range locally farmed duck livers that are actually very cheap to buy – much the same as chicken livers. I usually order my duck livers (flash-frozen) from Wild Peacock, a premium food distributor based in Stellenbosch that supplies many of the restaurants in the Western Cape with all kinds of products.

This duck liver terrine/parfait is all about the delicate texture and preserving some of the beautiful pink colour – don't overcook it or you'll be left with a grey liver-brick.

Note: The livers need to soak in milk overnight, so if you're planning on serving this for lunch on a Sunday, keep in mind that you need to soak them on the Friday evening before, cook it on the Saturday, and still have plenty of time for cooling and refrigeration overnight. In fact, it's a fabulous do-ahead dish as part of a more extensive feast – just unmould, garnish and serve.

Serves 10–12

1 kg free-range duck livers (thawed and rinsed, if frozen)
500 ml (2 cups) milk
2.5 ml (½ teaspoon) fine salt
1 clove garlic, finely chopped
½ small/medium onion, finely chopped
10 ml (2 teaspoons) fresh thyme leaves (no woody stalks)
125 ml (½ cup) brandy
125 ml (½ cup) port
250 g butter, melted
3 extra-large eggs
7.5 ml (1½ teaspoons) fine salt
2.5 ml (½ teaspoon) white pepper
bread, micro herbs, chutney, pickles and preserves (for serving)

Two days before serving: Soak the livers overnight in the milk and 2.5 ml (½ teaspoon) salt in a covered glass or ceramic bowl – this will help to reduce any bitterness.

The day before serving: Place the garlic and onion in a wide saucepan with the thyme, brandy and port. Bring to a boil, reducing the liquid until you have approximately 100 ml remaining. Set aside to cool for a few minutes.

Continued on following page

Continued from previous page

Drain and rinse the duck livers, then transfer them to a food processor or high-powered blender with the onion reduction (solids and liquid), melted butter, eggs, 7.5 ml (1½ teaspoons) salt and pepper. Process to a smooth pulp. Pass the mixture through a sieve (not too fine) to get rid of any stringy bits. Note: The mixture will be quite runny.

Preheat the oven to 130 °C. Line a terrine mould or loaf tin 30 x 11 x 7 cm (sprayed with non-stick cooking spray) with non-stick baking paper and spray the inside with non-stick spray. Pour in the liver mixture – it should come just to the top. Put a layer of baking paper on top of the mixture, then place the tin carefully in a larger deep baking tray and fill the larger tray with water to come two-thirds up the sides of the terrine. Bake the terrine in the water bath for 40–45 minutes. To check if it is done, insert a thermometer – the parfait should be 63–65 °C in the centre. If you don't have a thermostat, just bake it for 45 minutes to be safe.

Remove carefully from the oven, then remove from the water bath and allow to cool to room temperature before refrigerating overnight.

To serve: Carefully remove the top layer of baking paper. Run a knife around the sides of the tin (between the tin and the baking paper), then unmould the duck liver parfait onto a serving platter and remove the remaining baking paper. Garnish with pickles, preserves and micro herbs. To serve, slice 1.5 cm-thick slices using a hot sharp knife and serve with toasted bread, chutney, pickles and preserves/chutney.

This duck liver parfait makes such an elegant, 'grown up' starter with its delicate flavour and silky texture. Although the method may seem technical, it's really not difficult to make. The ingredients are relatively simple and inexpensive if you already have brandy and port on your shelf. If you're using a wider, shorter tin than the suggested size, add 5–10 minutes to the baking time.

hot-smoked trout terrine lined with cold-smoked trout ribbons

There's just something magical about a beautiful coral-coloured terrine – it's an instant celebration. This festive loaf is lined with delicate cold-smoked trout ribbons and filled with a creamy mixture of flaked cooked trout, fresh cream and lots of herbs. This terrine is not cheap to make, but it will feed a crowd and has received rave reviews every time I have served it. This makes an elegant yet laid-back starter, served with crisp melba toasts or crackers and a few lemon wedges. If you prefer a smoky flavour, use hot-smoked trout for the filling (if you're a progressive cook, you might even have the tools to smoke the fish at home), but for a milder flavour you can opt for poached/steamed/grilled trout.

Note: This terrine needs at least 4 hours to set in the fridge. It is a good choice to make it a day ahead of serving.

Serves 10–12

5 ml (1 teaspoon) canola oil (for brushing inside of terrine tin)
200 g cold-smoked trout ribbons
200 ml (¾ cup) chicken stock
20 ml (4 teaspoons) gelatine powder
3 x 250 ml (3 cups, roughly 180 g) deboned flaked trout (cooked or hot smoked, skin and bones removed)
juice of 1 medium lemon
230 g plain cream cheese
a large handful chopped fresh herbs (chives/dill/parsley)
salt and freshly ground black pepper
125 ml (½ cup) fresh cream, whipped
lemon wedges, melba toasts or crackers, to serve
capers, dill or watercress, for garnishing (optional)

Use a pastry brush to oil the inside of a classic terrine dish or a 21 x 11 x 7 cm loaf tin (this will make the turning out process a lot easier later). Line the inside of the tin with plastic wrap – leave the excess to hang over the sides, for folding over later.

Use ribbons of cold-smoked trout to carefully line the inside of the tin in the width, slightly overlapping to create a continuous effect (leave two or three for covering the top at the end).

Pour the cold chicken stock into a small saucepan, then add the gelatine powder and stir to combine. Leave to sponge for 10 minutes, then heat gently on the stovetop and stir until the gelatine has dissolved completely – do not boil. Set aside to cool slightly.

In a food processor, add the flaked trout, lemon juice, cream cheese and herbs. Now add the still slightly warm gelatine mixture and process to combine. Season generously with salt and pepper, then mix well. Taste and adjust seasoning, if necessary.

Transfer the mixture to a large mixing bowl, then lightly fold in the whipped cream until thoroughly mixed. Pour the terrine mixture into the trout-lined tin and use a spatula to smooth the top.

Cover the mixture with the remaining trout ribbons, then carefully fold the overhanging plastic wrap over the terrine. Use more plastic wrap to cover the top of the terrine, then place in the refrigerator to set for at least 4 hours, or preferably overnight.

To serve, remove the top layer of plastic wrap and unfold the sides of the wrap. Turn out onto a serving board, then carefully remove the tin (tug at the edges of the wrapping, it should slide out easily) and remove the remaining plastic wrap. Sprinkle with more chopped herbs and a handful of capers, and serve with lemon wedges and your choice of toast or crackers.

arancini with smoked mozzarella & aïoli

Of all the canapés that I've made and served in my lifetime, these little golden balls of delight are always scooped up first. They originated in Italy as a way to use up leftover risotto – the cold rice mixture is rolled into balls, stuffed with smoky cheese, crumbed and deep-fried. To add to the decadence, I serve it with a tangy garlic mayo. You can never get enough of it!

Note: Chilled risotto handles more easily than room temperature, so use the leftover risotto straight from the fridge. Assemble and re-refrigerate the balls in advance (with crumbs galore), then deep-fry just before serving.

Serves 6 as a snack/canapé

Aïoli (garlic mayonnaise)
2 egg yolks
1 clove garlic, peeled
5 ml (1 teaspoon) Dijon mustard
30 ml (2 tablespoons) freshly squeezed lemon juice or apple cider vinegar
salt and freshly ground black pepper
180–250 ml (⅔–1 cup) canola oil

Arancini
about 500 ml (2 cups) prepared leftover risotto, chilled (any flavour will do, page 149)
100 g smoked mozzarella, cut into 1 cm cubes
125 ml (½ cup) flour
salt and freshly ground black pepper
3 eggs, lightly whisked
500 ml (2 cups) fresh breadcrumbs
750 ml (3 cups) canola oil

For the aïoli, place the yolks, garlic, mustard and lemon juice in a blender or food processor. Season with salt and pepper, then blend well. With the motor running, add the oil in a thin stream until fully incorporated and thick and creamy. Transfer to a glass jar and refrigerate until ready to use.

For the arancini, take a small tablespoon of cold risotto and insert a cube of mozzarella. Shape the risotto to cover the cheese and roll it into a neat ball (cold risotto is easier to shape). Continue until all the risotto is used.

In a shallow bowl, mix the flour with some salt and pepper. Place the breadcrumbs in another shallow bowl, and the eggs in yet another.

Dip each risotto ball into the seasoned flour, then into the egg and then into the breadcrumbs, covering it all over. Place on a clean plate and repeat.

Heat the oil to about 180 °C, then fry batches of arancini until golden all over – about 3 minutes. Serve with the aïoli.

For a more formal way of serving, use a small plastic bag to pipe blobs of aïoli in neat rows onto a serving board, then 'stick' the arancini onto each piped blob to keep them from rolling around.

CHAPTER 4:

soups, chowders & stews

trout & fennel chowder

This is a great way of stretching a fillet of trout to feed six people in style! This chowder should be quite chunky, so don't try to cook the potatoes down to a mushy pulp – they should be just tender enough to break apart when applying light pressure. Fresh dill and a squeeze of lemon juice provide the perfect zesty finishing touches to a creamy, hearty chowder.

Serves 6

250 ml (1 cup) dry white wine
about 300 g trout fillet/s (skinless and boneless)
30 g butter
15 ml (1 tablespoon) extra virgin olive oil
1 medium-size fennel bulb, rinsed and finely sliced
1 white onion, finely chopped
2 cloves garlic, finely chopped
3 large (about 600 g) potatoes, peeled and diced into small cubes (roughly 1 cm)
500 ml (2 cups) chicken stock
250 ml (1 cup) fresh cream
salt and freshly ground black pepper
finely grated rind of ½ lemon
a generous handful fresh dill, chopped (or chives or parsley)

Place the wine and trout in a pot with a lid and bring to a simmer. Simmer/steam for about 5 minutes until the fish is just cooked. Remove the fish, reserving the wine. Flake the fish and set aside.

Heat the butter and olive oil in a large wide pot over medium heat. Fry the fennel and onion until soft and lightly golden (not brown). Add the garlic and stir for another minute. Add the potatoes, chicken stock and reserved wine. Bring to a simmer, turn the heat down to low and cook for about 20 minutes, or until the potatoes are tender. Add the flaked fish and cream and heat through, stirring. Season generously with salt and pepper, then add the lemon rind and half the herbs. Remove from the heat and stir, then leave to stand for 10–15 minutes to thicken slightly.

Serve hot in bowls topped with more chopped herbs and, optionally, some crusty bread.

Fennel bulbs are usually in season during spring. If you cannot find any, use leeks instead. Also, if you want to substitute the potatoes, use chopped cauliflower.

mussel & tomato stew

This recipe has its roots in the beginnings of a Spanish paella. I've made dozens of paellas in my lifetime, and one of the secrets to a deeply flavoured dish is to take your time with frying the onions, tomatoes and red pepper (and chorizo, in the case of paella) until it intensifies in colour and becomes really soft and dark. Although chorizo is a fantastic ingredient, it can be pricy. Using smoked paprika in its place for this stew will bring even more deep red tones to it – you'll only use a tablespoon and the stew will have a fantastic smoky undertone. Smoked paprika is such a stunning, versatile ingredient, I never go without it in my kitchen.

Note: This recipe needs fresh live black mussels – frozen just won't do. Order yours from Blue Ocean Mussels. Also, if tomatoes aren't in season, you're welcome to use 1–2 cans whole Italian tomatoes, chopped (not the canned chopped tomatoes – they sometimes taste artificial).

Serves 6

In a very big, wide, heavy-bottomed pan (30 cm cast-iron or enamelled cast-iron works very well), heat the oil over medium heat and fry the onion, red pepper and garlic until just soft. Add the tomatoes and paprika, then turn up the heat and fry for 10–15 minutes, stirring often, until the tomatoes break up and start to go darker and sticky on the bottom. Add the wine, stir and bring to a boil. Add the mussels, cover with a lid and steam for 8–10 minutes, or until the mussels are all open (discard any that haven't opened). Stir well – the mussels will release their salty sea water, so don't season the stew until you've cooked the mussels and tasted for salt levels. Season with salt (if necessary) and pepper, then sprinkle with the herbs and serve immediately with some crusty bread on the side to dip into the sauce.

cape seafood stew (cape-style bouillabaisse)

This legendary seafood dish is right up there with a few others that make up my favourite foods of all time.

There are so many traditional ways of making a proper bouillabaisse, and most true recipes take quite a bit of effort and time (some take days). I've found that the only way to do it is with really fresh seafood (especially the fish and prawns) and to go the extra mile and make your own stock too, using the fish bones and prawn heads – it makes a huge difference. A dark seafood stock is what you're aiming for, and roasting the prawn heads gives great colour and depth of flavour.

I've broken the prep into four stages. I know it looks like a massive job, but trust me, there's a reason for every single ingredient and method on this list and it will reward you deeply. Serve the stew with toasted bread spread with thick Aïoli (garlic mayonnaise, page 80).

Serves 6–8

Phase 1: Prepare the seafood
1.8–2 kg fresh whole fish (yellowtail, dorado etc. – firm white wish, not oily fish)
400–500 g whole prawns (medium-large), thawed
15–30 ml (1–2 tablespoons) extra virgin olive oil
1–1.2kg fresh live black mussels

Preheat the oven to 220 °C.

Ask your fishmonger to gill and gut the fish, and to fillet it neatly (if you can do this yourself, well done!). Keep the bones and heads separate for making stock.

Twist the heads off the raw prawns, remove the shells on the tails and spread the heads and shells out on a baking tray and drizzle lightly with olive oil. Roast for about 15 minutes until brown on the edges, then set aside.

Clean the mussels (scrub, rinse and debeard) while you are making the stock in the next phase.

Continued on following page

Saffron is a relatively expensive ingredient, but I love the distinctive pungency it brings. Buy small quantities at good spice shops like Atlas Spices in Cape Town or Radis Spices in Stellenbosch – this way it won't cost you an arm and a leg, but you'll have enough for one recipe.

Continued from previous page

Phase 2: Prepare the stock (can be done a day ahead)
1.5 litres (6 cups) water
2 good quality chicken stock cubes, crumbled (optional, but it helps to create a richer stock)
fresh fish bones and heads (see phase 1)
roasted prawn heads and shells with pan juices (see phase 1)
2 onions, halved (skin on)
2 carrots, cut into large chunks (skin on)
1 stalk celery, cut into chunks
2 whole garlic cloves (skin on)
a few fresh parsley stalks
2.5 ml (½ teaspoon) whole black peppercorns
1 bay leaf

Place all the ingredients in a large stock pot and bring to a boil. Simmer over moderate heat for 30 minutes, then remove from the heat and let it stand, uncovered, for another 30 minutes. Strain the liquid into another pot (keep aside) and discard the solids. (If making ahead, let the stock cool to room temperature, then transfer to a plastic container with lid and refrigerate until ready to use.)

Phase 3: Prepare the aïoli (garlic mayonnaise)

You can obviously cheat here and just mix 200 ml (¾ cup) good quality store-bought mayo with 1 clove finely grated garlic, or you can go the whole nine yards and make your own. See page 80.

Phase 4: The stew
60 ml (¼ cup) extra virgin olive oil
1 onion, peeled and finely chopped
1 stalk celery, finely chopped
1 large carrot, peeled and finely chopped
4 cloves garlic, finely chopped or grated
15 ml (1 tablespoon) tomato paste
375 ml (½ bottle) unwooded dry white wine, such as sauvignon/chenin blanc
30 ml (2 tablespoons) Cape brandy
a pinch saffron
peeled rind from 1 orange (no pith)
1 bay leaf
1 can (400 g) whole peeled tomatoes, finely puréed in a blender
about 1.25 litres (5 cups) fish stock (see phase 2)
about 500 g fresh fish fillets, cut into smaller chunks (see phase 1)
about 250 g shelled prawn tail meat (see phase 1)
1–1.2 kg fresh black mussels, cleaned (see phase 1)
salt and freshly ground black pepper
a bunch fresh parsley (or fresh dill), roughly chopped, to serve
1 or 2 baguettes, sliced and toasted, to serve
aïoli (garlic mayonnaise), to serve (see phase 3)

Heat the oil in a big, wide, heavy-bottomed pot (30 cm Le Creuset casserole works well). Fry the onion, celery, carrot and garlic over medium heat until soft, but not brown. Add the tomato paste and keep frying until it darkens in colour (2–3 minutes). Add the wine, brandy, saffron, orange rind, bay leaf, canned tomatoes and fish stock. Turn the heat up to high and bring to a boil, stirring to loosen any sticky bits on the bottom. Cook for 10 minutes, then add the fish fillets, prawn meat and mussels. Bring to a boil again, then cook for about 8 minutes or until the seafood is just cooked and the mussels are open. Taste and add salt and pepper to taste, then remove from the heat. Drizzle with a little more olive oil, then serve in bowls topped with fresh parsley or dill and toasted baguette spread with a dollop of aïoli.

split pea soup
with smoked pork & cape tawny

This recipe is one of the simplest out there and just delivers on flavour and comfort every single time. With one packet of split peas, a few smoked pork steaks, onions, beef stock cubes and a splash of sherry (or Cape Tawny, as it is known these days), you'll get much more than you bargained for. In earlier years, I made this recipe using smoked pork hocks, but recently I've switched to smoked boneless pork steaks – easier to handle and quicker to cook. Inexpensive comfort food doesn't get better than this.

Note: There are two great pork butcheries in my neck of the woods: Joostenberg and Sweetwell. They're both well worth a visit and sell exceptional quality pork products at great prices. Pork is my favourite type of meat, without a doubt.

Serves 6

2.5 litres (10 cups) water
3 beef stock cubes
1 packet (500 g) split peas
4 smoked pork neck steaks (boneless), cut into 1 cm cubes
2 onions, finely chopped
salt and freshly ground black pepper
about 30 ml (2 tablespoons) Cape tawny (or sherry)
freshly baked bread, to serve (optional)

Place the water, stock cubes, peas, pork cubes and onions in a large stock pot and bring to a boil (yes, no frying necessary). Cook for approximately 2½ hours, or until the split peas are completely soft and the soup thickens (stir now and then to prevent sticking). Add salt and pepper to taste and then a splash of Cape Tawny for some welcome wintery sweetness. Serve hot in bowls, with bread to dip.

This soup will continue to thicken on standing, and will become almost scoopable when refrigerated. Add a splash of water to thin any leftovers upon reheating, if necessary.

chicken, chickpea & couscous soup with cumin & fresh mint

This recipe was inspired originally by a canned soup that I used to buy in my early twenties from Woolworths. I had just moved into a place of my own and often bought this delicious Moroccan chicken and chickpea soup as a quick dinner fix before going out to party with friends – we never went out for dinner, we only went out for 'extended drinks'. When it was discontinued, I felt heartbroken (don't laugh, it was a long time ago). So, in my thirties, I tried to recreate this lovely soup from memory and I think I got pretty close. It is remarkably simple – although the list of ingredients seems long – and mostly consists of trusted pantry staples. I love the textural variety between the soft chicken and the slightly firmer chickpeas. The couscous is added right at the end and just gives added body – trust me, it works.

This is a hearty midweek dinner, and creates the best leftovers for lunch the next day (also great as breakfast after a proper party the night before).

Serves 4–6

1 medium-size chicken (without giblets)
45 ml (3 tablespoons) extra virgin olive oil
2 onions, chopped
3 cloves garlic, finely chopped
5 ml (1 teaspoon) ground cumin
5 ml (1 teaspoon) ground coriander
10 ml (2 teaspoons) smoked paprika
1 stick cinnamon
5–10 ml (1–2 teaspoons) harissa paste (page 43), depending on how hot you like it
1.5 litres (6 cups) chicken stock
1 can (400 g) whole Italian tomatoes, puréed
salt and freshly ground black pepper
1 can (400 g) chickpeas, drained
250 ml (1 cup) uncooked couscous
a handful fresh mint, finely chopped (or coriander or parsley)
about 125 ml (½ cup) plain yoghurt, to serve (optional)
fresh lemon wedges, to serve (optional)

Using a large chef's knife or poultry shears, cut the chicken into quarters (or roughly into large chunks). Heat the oil in a large, wide pot and fry the chicken pieces on all sides until golden. Remove from the pot and turn the heat down to medium. Add the onions and fry until soft and translucent. Add the garlic, cumin, coriander, paprika, cinnamon stick and harissa and fry for a minute or two, stirring. Add the stock and tomatoes and stir to loosen any sticky bits on the bottom of the pot. Return the chicken pieces to the pot, cover with a lid and bring to a boil. Reduce to a slow simmer and cook for about 1 hour until the chicken is very tender and falls from the bone. Remove from the heat, then remove the chicken pieces with tongs and debone them, discarding the bones and shredding the meat. Place the shredded meat back into the pot. Season the soup with salt and pepper and add the chickpeas and couscous. Reheat to a simmer, then cook for about 5 minutes, or until the couscous is tender. Stir in a handful chopped mint, then serve hot topped with more mint and, optionally, a dollop of plain yoghurt and fresh lemon wedges.

italian-style white bean soup with karoo lamb & white wine

I wrote this recipe for my friends at Lamb and Mutton South Africa as part of a 'Fresh take on Winter' series, and they've agreed to share it in my book. This recipe uses white haricot beans (almost like Italian cannellini beans) available in most supermarkets in bags labelled 'small white beans'. They are very smooth in texture and do not fall apart as easily as their red speckled cousins, resulting in a non-stodgy, slightly thickened brothy soup with chunks of deliciously tender meat. Made with chicken stock and white wine instead of mutton/beef stock, the soup is also lighter in colour and just looks 'fresher'. A dollop of punchy green salsa verde adds just the right kick. A single lamb knuckle, sliced by your butcher, is enough to add the meatiness that this soup needs. It's an economical way of serving a stylish soup in a fresh way. Serve with crusty bread, if you like.

Serves 6

30 ml (2 tablespoons) extra virgin olive oil
about 600 g lamb knuckle, sliced horizontally by your butcher
1 large onion, finely chopped
1–2 stalks celery, finely chopped
1 large (or 2 medium-size) carrots, peeled and finely chopped
3 cloves garlic, finely chopped
3 sprigs fresh rosemary
250 ml (1 cup) dry white wine
2 litres (8 cups) chicken stock
500 g small white (haricot) beans
salt and freshly ground black pepper
bread, for serving (optional)

Salsa verde
a handful each fresh parsley, basil and mint
1 clove garlic, peeled
10 ml (2 teaspoons) capers
15–30 ml (1–2 tablespoons) freshly squeezed lemon juice
45–60 ml (3–4 tablespoons) extra virgin olive oil
a pinch fine salt
10 ml (2 teaspoons) Dijon mustard

To make the soup, heat the oil over high heat in a large pot (at least 6 litres capacity), then fry the lamb (cut larger chunks in half) in batches until browned on both sides. Remove the meat from the pot and set aside, then turn down the heat to medium. Don't season the meat yet, otherwise the beans will not soften.

Add the onion, celery and carrots to the same pot and fry until soft, stirring often (add a little more oil if needed). Add the garlic and rosemary (add the sprigs whole, you can remove the woody stems later) and fry for another minute. The bottom of the pot should be coated with sticky brown bits by now. Add the wine and stir to deglaze.

Return the fried meat with all the juices to the pot, then add the stock and beans and stir. Cover with a lid, bring to a simmer, then turn the heat down to low and cook for 2½–3 hours until the meat is falling from the bones and the beans are really tender.

Season well with salt and pepper. Remove from the heat and rest for about 15 minutes before serving.

To make the salsa verde, chop all the ingredients together by hand or in a food processor. Taste and adjust with more salt or lemon juice if needed. Serve the soup in bowls with a dollop of salsa verde (and some crusty bread for dipping, optionally).

roasted tomato soup
with garlic & thyme

In the height of summer, you can sometimes find large boxes of tomatoes at some retailers and vegetable stands. Look for the box with the ripest tomatoes – they don't have to be perfect, they just need to be bright red and ripe, slightly tender to the touch. If you have access to tomatoes straight from a farm that are really ripe and have not seen the inside of a fridge, those are first prize (my friends at Genesis Farm outside Stellenbosch grow some pretty amazing tomatoes). Under ripe, pale, firm tomatoes that are out of season make a far inferior soup, so don't even try it.

The aroma of this soup roasting in the oven is unlike anything else – so deeply flavoursome and intensely umami-rich. Remember that the tomatoes will reduce quite a bit – almost by half – so don't be afraid to start with a really big load.

Note: To save time, process the leeks, onion, carrot and garlic together in a food processor before frying. Also, pulse the tomatoes in batches in a food processor if you don't want to do it by hand.

Serves 4–6

45 ml (3 tablespoons) extra virgin olive oil
a small bunch (about 200 g) leeks, finely chopped
1 onion, finely chopped
1 large carrot, finely chopped
4 cloves garlic, finely chopped
6–8 sprigs thyme, woody stalks discarded (or about 2 tablespoons fresh thyme leaves)
about 2 kg ripe organic tomatoes, chopped into chunks
2 cans (400 g each) whole Italian tomatoes, chopped into chunks
30 ml (2 tablespoons) sugar
15 ml (1 tablespoon) fine salt
10 ml (2 teaspoons) freshly ground black pepper
30 ml (2 tablespoons) red wine vinegar
10 ml (2 teaspoons) balsamic vinegar
125 ml (½ cup) fresh cream (optional)
fresh basil leaves and extra virgin olive oil, to serve
fresh rustic bread, for dipping

Preheat the oven to 180 °C.

In a large, wide, cast-iron pot (one that can also go into the oven) on the stovetop, heat the olive oil, then fry the leeks, onion, carrot, garlic and thyme until soft and golden.

Add the tomatoes (fresh and canned), as well as the sugar, salt, pepper and vinegars. Stir well then roast in the oven, uncovered, for 1½ hours (stir every 30 minutes).

Remove from the oven, then optionally use a stick blender to process to the desired consistency – sometimes I prefer it chunkier, other times I like it smoother. Stir in the cream (if using), adjust the seasoning if necessary and serve with a few basil leaves and a drizzle of extra virgin olive oil, with some bread on the side.

creamed cauliflower with brown butter & gruyère cheese

Cauliflower was probably the most boring (yet dependable) vegetable when I grew up, although I've always liked it. Boiled in water and covered in cheese sauce, it was a midweek staple in our house. In the more recent era of banting, this humble pale vegetable became a superstar because of its low carbohydrate content and versatility in cooking.

My absolute favourite way of serving cauliflower is as a silky purée – it is spectacular as a substitute for mashed potatoes with shreds of saucy meat or pan-fried fish on top, but it also serves as a creamy velouté-style sauce. You can serve this recipe as a soup-type starter topped with a drizzle of brown butter and shavings of local Gruyère-style cheese, or you can use it as a 'bed' for serving many other dishes over it. The secret is that you need to boil the cauliflower IN the cream – don't just add it later. Something magical happens this way, and I don't really know why. The flavour is really intense and the texture is absolutely grain free and silky. It is so very simple, but incredibly delicious.

Serves 4–6

1 large head cauliflower
250 ml (1 cup) fresh cream
a generous pinch fine salt

Brown butter
125 g butter

For serving
a few shavings of mature Gruyère-style cheese (Kleinrivier Gruberg or Dalewood Huguenot work very well)

Cut the cauliflower into smaller florets (discard the green leaves on the bottom, but use the whole head) and place in a medium-size pot. Add the cream and salt and bring to a boil. Turn the heat down to a simmer and cover with a lid so that the cauliflower can steam and cook at the same time, taking care that the cream doesn't boil over – watch it carefully. Cook until tender but not mushy, about 10 minutes. Remove from the heat, then transfer the cooked cauliflower and half the hot cream to a blender or food processor. Process until very smooth and silky – add more hot cream to make it runnier (if serving as a soup-style starter, add all the cream). Adjust the seasoning and set aside.

To make the brown butter, melt the butter in a small saucepan over medium-high heat. Keep on cooking until it bubbles, swirling the saucepan every now and then. After 5–7 minutes the butter will start to foam and it will release some golden brown bits on the bottom and a wonderfully nutty flavour. Remove from the heat and keep swirling until the foaming subsides, then set aside.

Serve the hot cauliflower purée with a drizzle of brown butter and a few shavings of cheese.

leek & potato soup
with mature gouda cheese

A few years ago, I was asked to cook and serve tasters at a Cape Town food festival for Potatoes South Africa. One of the tasters was a fantastic creamy potato soup with buttery leeks (the other was spicy curried potatoes – also a hit). Over the course of three days, we served almost a hundred litres of that soup in small tasting portions, and the people at the festival absolutely loved it. It has since become a firm favourite in my soup repertoire, and makes an elegant starter for a dinner party.

A local mature Gouda and a drizzle of brown butter add a deep nuttiness to the soup. It's a crowd pleaser every single time, made with relatively few, simple ingredients.

Serves 6

125 g butter
2 bunches leeks, white parts only, finely sliced (4–5 cups)
1 onion, finely chopped
4 large potatoes, peeled and cubed (about 1 cm)
1 litre (4 cups) vegetable stock
250 ml (1 cup) fresh cream
at least 100 g mature Gouda (about 250ml/1 cup grated)
salt and freshly ground black pepper
brown butter, to serve (page 100)
bread, for dipping (optional)

In a large stock pot or heavy-bottomed pot, melt the butter over medium heat and add the leeks and onion. Fry, stirring, until very soft but not brown – don't rush, it might take up to 15 minutes.

Add the potatoes and stock and bring to a simmer. Cook for about 30 minutes or until the potato cubes are very tender and start to fall apart. Remove from the heat, then use a stick blender to process the soup to a smooth purée (or transfer to a blender).

Put the pot back on the heat and add the cream and Gouda. Stir until the cheese has melted and the soup is warmed through (do not boil again). Season with salt and pepper, then serve hot in bowls with a drizzle of warm brown butter and a light grinding of black pepper.

salads, vegetables & legumes

caprese salad with buffalo mozzarella & aged balsamic vinegar

There's a water buffalo dairy farm outside Wellington, called Buffalo Ridge. They are the only local producers of buffalo mozzarella in South Africa, and one of only a handful in the world that produce authentic *mozzarella di bufala* outside of Campania, Italy (a highly regulated industry).

Water buffalo milk contains a butter fat percentage far in excess of that of cow's milk. It has substantially higher levels of protein, calcium, natural antioxidants and natural preservatives (and it's naturally low in cholesterol), which allows the production of stretched mozzarella without the use of additives and chemicals. Although more expensive than its well-known cow's milk cousin (*fior di latte*), it is a superb product that should be celebrated and savoured.

The absolute best way of enjoying *mozzarella di bufala* is with perfectly ripe beefy tomatoes, a few basil leaves, the best quality extra virgin olive oil you can find, and a few drops of aged balsamic vinegar like Rozendal's 20-year-old Essentia. These special ingredients elevate a regular Caprese salad to food from the heavens – simply unforgettable.

Serves 2 – adapt quantities accordingly

2 ripe beef tomatoes, thickly sliced
125 g *mozzarella di bufala*, torn into chunky shreds
a few basil leaves
salt flakes and freshly ground black pepper
a drizzle of the finest extra virgin olive oil
a few drops of aged balsamic vinegar

Arrange the sliced tomatoes and chunks of mozzarella on plates, then top with basil leaves, season with salt and pepper, and drizzle with olive oil and a few drops of aged balsamic vinegar.

fennel, celery & granny smith apple salad

I made this salad for the first time in 2013 as part of a Christmas shoot, with roasted trout and crushed buttery pan-fried potatoes. Apart from slicing off the tip of my finger with a mandoline cutter (a painful mistake I have not made since), the day will be remembered for the way everyone at the shoot raved about the salad. I have made this salad so many times I cannot count, and every single time someone asks for the recipe. It is deceptively simple, containing only three ingredients (apart from the dressing). Its magic lies in the textural crunch, and the beautiful play between fresh, sweet and zesty.

Serves 6 as a side dish

2 large fennel bulbs, rinsed
2 long stalks celery
1 large green apple (Granny Smith)
about 15 ml (1 tablespoon) freshly squeezed lemon juice
30 ml (2 tablespoons) extra virgin olive oil
10 ml (2 teaspoons) wholegrain mustard
salt and freshly ground black pepper

Slice the fennel bulbs horizontally (at a slight angle) into very fine shavings, preferably using a mandoline cutter on a very thin setting. Finely slice some of the fennel fronds as well (about 250 ml/1 cup), and place it all in a large salad bowl.

Slice the celery finely with the mandoline cutter. Cut the apple into fine julienne strips (do not peel). Add both to the bowl.

Mix the lemon juice, olive oil and mustard in a small mixing bowl, then pour it over the salad. Season with salt and pepper, then toss it all together until coated all over with the dressing. Serve immediately, or cover and refrigerate until ready to serve (see notes below).

The salad is best sliced by hand with a mandoline cutter (just be careful, because you cannot really use the protective cover while holding the fennel at an angle) rather than in a food processor. The salad is also best eaten immediately, or within an hour or two after preparing (if chilled) – the dressing will continue to wilt the ingredients on standing, but prevents the apple from turning brown.

roasted root vegetable salad
with lemon & goat's milk cheese

This is a superb vegetarian dish – satisfying on so many levels and best served lukewarm or at room temperature. The lentils are earthy and nutty, the goat's milk cheese is creamy and punchy, and the vegetables are slightly charred and tender.

Serves 4 as a main meal or 6 as a side dish

Lentils
250 g (2 cups) brown or black lentils
water, to cover
45 ml (3 tablespoons) extra virgin olive oil
juice and finely grated rind of 1 medium-size lemon
1 clove garlic, finely grated
10 ml (2 teaspoons) honey
salt and freshly ground black pepper
a small bunch fresh Italian parsley and mint, finely chopped

Roasted vegetables
assorted vegetables, peeled and cut into bite-size chunks (like beetroot, carrots, Brussels sprouts and leeks – enough to fill a standard roasting tray in a single layer)
30 ml (2 tablespoons) extra virgin olive oil
2.5 ml (½ teaspoon) ground cumin
2.5 ml (½ teaspoon) ground cinnamon
salt and freshly ground black pepper

To assemble
200 g plain goat's milk cheese (chevin)
more parsley and mint, roughly chopped, to serve
about 30 ml (2 tablespoons) pine nuts (or flaked almonds), roasted in a dry pan

For the lentils, place them in a large pot and cover with cold water (about 5 cm above the lentils). Cook for about 30 minutes until tender but still retaining shape, then drain and rinse briefly with hot water. Shake off excess water, then transfer to a large mixing bowl. Mix the olive oil, lemon juice and rind, garlic and honey in a small mixing bowl, then pour it over the warm lentils and season generously with salt and pepper. Add the parsley and mint and stir well.

For the vegetables, preheat the oven to 220 °C. Arrange the vegetables on a roasting tray, drizzle with oil and season with cumin, cinnamon, salt and pepper. Roast for 30 minutes or until golden brown and tender.

To assemble: Add the roasted veg to the cooked lentils, add chunks of goat's milk cheese, then scatter with more parsley, mint and pine nuts. Serve warm or at room temperature.

green on green salad: broccolini, avo & asparagus with poached eggs & 'green goddess' dressing

When I think about my favourite salads, they are mostly topped with avocado and eggs, and some kind of luscious dressing. It's the moreish mouthfeel that I'm after – soft and creamy and rich, with a pop of texture and crunch in between provided by fresh greens or seeds or nuts or even croutons. It leaves me utterly satisfied and happy.

This green on green salad is so versatile and beautiful, and can be enjoyed as a meal on its own or as part of a large festive spread. Use whatever greens you love – crunchy mange tout works like a charm, as well as shaved raw baby marrow, blanched green beans, and so on.

Serves 6 as a side dish

Salad
200 g broccolini spears, sliced diagonally into shorter spears
4–6 medium/large fresh free-range eggs
200 g mixed baby greens (baby spinach, rocket, watercress, etc.)
a small bunch green asparagus (choose thin spears, preferably), sliced diagonally into shorter chunks
2 ripe avocados, peeled, pip removed, sliced

Green goddess dressing
60 ml (¼ cup) good-quality mayonnaise
60 ml (¼ cup) double cream plain yoghurt
15 ml (1 tablespoon) Dijon mustard
30 ml (2 tablespoons) freshly squeezed lemon juice
15 ml (1 tablespoon) extra virgin olive oil
a handful fresh dill, chopped
a handful fresh Italian parsley, chopped
a handful fresh chives, chopped
salt and freshly ground black pepper

For the salad, blanch the broccolini for 2 minutes in 1 cm boiling water, covered. Remove and plunge into ice water, then set aside. Poach the eggs (in 5 cm deep simmering water with 15 ml/1 tablespoon vinegar added to the water) for about 4 minutes, then remove with a slotted spoon and set aside.

Arrange the baby greens on a large platter, then top with the blanched broccolini, raw sliced asparagus, avo and eggs. Use a sharp knife to cut into the centre of the eggs to release some of the oozing soft yolks.

For the dressing, place all the ingredients in a food processer and process to a smooth green pulp. Adjust seasoning and mix well. If you need to thin it slightly, add a tablespoon or two of cold water and mix well.

Drizzle the dressing all over the salad, then season with salt and pepper. Serve at once.

Using very fresh eggs helps when you want to poach them, in that the egg white stays 'together'. The egg white from older eggs tends to go runny and they are much more difficult to poach neatly.

cape caesar salad with ciabatta croutons

I'm of the opinion that you can judge any food establishment by their Caesar salad. I always order it if displayed on a menu. There's a fine line between a nice Caesar salad and a great one. To me, it lies in the detail, but also in restraint and simplicity: less is more. So, make a killer dressing and make sure you choose only the freshest, crunchy, small heads of cos lettuce. Coat the leaves generously, then you pretty much won't need anything else, except for a few crunchy golden croutons and a few shavings of aged Parmesan. Heavenly.

Serves 4

Dressing
2 extra-large egg yolks
30 ml (2 tablespoons) apple cider vinegar
2 anchovy fillets (preserved in oil), chopped
1 clove garlic, chopped or grated
10 ml (2 teaspoons) Dijon mustard
5 ml (1 teaspoon) Worcestershire sauce
45 ml (3 tablespoons) finely grated Parmigiano-Reggiano (Parmesan)
salt and freshly ground black pepper
60 ml (¼ cup) canola oil

Salad
2–3 slices good-quality ciabatta, torn into small chunks
60 ml (¼ cup) extra virgin olive oil
salt and freshly ground black pepper
2 small heads cos lettuce (or baby gem lettuce)
about 50 g aged Parmesan, shaved

For the dressing, place the yolks, vinegar, anchovies, garlic, mustard, Worcestershire sauce and Parmesan in a tall cup. Using a stick blender, blend it well and season with salt and pepper. With the motor running, add the oil in a thin stream to produce a thickened sauce, continuing to blend until all the oil is incorporated. Season again with salt and pepper to taste and mix well.

For the croutons, place the bread chunks in a large non-stick pan over high heat. Drizzle all over with the olive oil and fry, stirring now and then, until golden all over. Season with salt and pepper and set aside.

To assemble, break the cos lettuce heads into individual leaves, then rinse and drain well. In a large bowl, toss the leaves with some of the dressing, then arrange on a large platter. Top with croutons and shaved Parmesan, and serve with more dressing on the side.

panzanella (bread salad) with sourdough croutons & red wine vinegar dressing

The first time I had a bread salad was at a neighbour's house for dinner, probably 10 years ago. Not only did I love the salad, I also learned that not all croutons are created equal. The quality of your panzanella is totally dependent on the quality of the bread you use, so choose a wood-fired sourdough loaf or rustic ciabatta made with unbleached stoneground flour and you're halfway there. Toast the bread chunks in a hot pan with olive oil (don't deep-fry) and you're left with toasty croutons that are crunchy and chewy, but still soft in the middle and can absorb the delicious dressing.

Note: Only assemble the salad when ready to serve otherwise the dressed croutons will become soggy.

Serves 6

Red wine vinegar dressing
60 ml (¼ cup) extra virgin olive oil
60 ml (¼ cup) red wine vinegar
1 clove garlic, finely grated
salt and freshly ground black pepper

Croutons
60 ml (¼ cup) extra virgin olive oil
3–4 x 250 ml (3–4 cups) bread chunks (cut bread into slices and tear into bite-size chunks)
salt and freshly ground black pepper

Salad
500–600 g ripe tomatoes (roma or rosa, or exotic mixed), cut into smaller chunks/cubes
1 yellow pepper, pith removed and thinly sliced (not chopped)
1 small to medium-size red onion, finely sliced (not chopped)
30–45 ml (2–3 tablespoons) small capers, drained
8 anchovy fillets in oil, drained and chopped (optional)
2 punnets (about 40 g) fresh basil (or half basil, half parsley)
1 batch croutons (see above)
1 batch dressing (see above)

For the dressing, place all the ingredients in a glass jar, cover with a lid and shake to mix.

For the croutons, heat the olive oil in a large non-stick pan over high heat and fry the bread chunks, tossing frequently, until golden brown. Season with salt and pepper and set aside to cool slightly.

For the salad, place the tomatoes, yellow pepper, onion, capers and anchovies in a large salad bowl. Remove the stalks of the basil (and optionally parsley) and add the whole leaves, broken up individually (roughly chopped if using parsley). Add the croutons and dressing, and toss to coat evenly – the croutons will absorb a lot of the dressing. Taste and add more salt and pepper, if necessary. Serve at once.

In Italy, croutons for panzanella are broken into pieces by hand, not cut. Although a little time-consuming, it does deliver the most authentic result.

tabbouleh (parsley, tomato & cucumber salad with bulgur wheat)

Tabbouleh has become somewhat of a global deli staple and can be found in so many South African shops that offer buffet-style lunches. It's incredibly fresh in flavour and texture, and is a phenomenal accompaniment to many other Mediterranean dishes (although traditionally eaten in the Middle East scooped up with small cos lettuce leaves).

When you're making your own, remember that tabbouleh is essentially a parsley salad, not a bulgur wheat salad. The main ingredient is parsley, then tomatoes, then bulgur wheat. Fine bulgur wheat is available in most health shops and can conveniently be soaked in cold water (no cooking needed). Coarse bulgur wheat needs cooking – follow instructions on packets, if using.

Serves 6

250 ml (1 cup) fine bulgur wheat
375 ml (1½ cups) cold water
salt and freshly ground black pepper
1 ml (¼ teaspoon) ground cinnamon
1 ml (¼ teaspoon) ground cumin
2.5 ml (½ teaspoon) ground allspice
375 ml (1½ cups) finely diced tomato
250 ml (1 cup) finely diced and seeded cucumber
4 punnets (80–100 g) fresh Italian or curly parsley, most stalks removed, finely chopped
1 punnet (20 g) fresh mint, stalks removed, finely sliced
1 bunch spring onions, finely sliced
60 ml (¼ cup) extra virgin olive oil
30 ml (2 tablespoons) freshly squeezed lemon juice

Place the bulgur and water in a medium-size mixing bowl and soak for 20 minutes. Drain very well and set aside – it won't be very soft yet, but will continue to absorb the juices of the salad later. Season generously with salt and pepper, then add the cinnamon, cumin, allspice, tomato, cucumber, parsley, mint and spring onions. Drizzle all over with the olive oil and lemon juice. Mix well, then cover and leave to stand for at least 30 minutes before serving (refrigerate during hot weather). Serve cold or at room temperature.

grilled aubergine & courgette salad with bocconcini & mint

A few years ago, I posted a shaved aubergine and courgette salad on my blog. Although it is super delicious, it is quite prep-intensive. I've since updated it as a chunkier al fresco version to be prepped over a fire, saving more than some time. Essentially, this salad is all about the charring, which brings magnificent flavour to two of my favourite vegetables. For best results, grill slices over hot coals until dark and smoky, then cut into smaller chunks and toss in a zippy dressing of olive oil, lemon juice, fresh garlic and mint. Serve with chunks of milky bocconcini and some fresh rocket.

Serves 6

Dressing
60 ml (¼ cup) extra virgin olive oil
30 ml (2 tablespoons) freshly squeezed lemon juice, plus some of the grated rind for topping
1 clove garlic, finely grated
a handful fresh mint, finely chopped, plus more to garnish
salt and freshly ground black pepper

Salad
1 large or 2 medium aubergines, sliced into 1-cm-thick rounds
200 g courgettes (baby marrows), halved lengthways
a bunch fresh rocket, washed and drained
250 g bocconcini (soft fresh mozzarella balls), sliced

For the dressing, place the olive oil, lemon juice, garlic and chopped mint in a glass jar, season generously with salt and pepper and shake to mix. Set aside.

For the salad, grill the sliced aubergines and courgettes on both sides over hot coals, using a grid and tongs to turn them over once charred. When ready, remove from the fire, then chop into bite-size chunks on a cutting board (don't burn yourself) and place in a bowl. Immediately pour the dressing over and stir to coat. The vegetables will absorb a lot of the dressing, so leave to stand for at least 15–30 minutes until cooled.

On a salad platter, arrange the rocket leaves, then top with the grilled dressed vegetables, some sliced bocconcini and a few mint leaves. Serve at room temperature.

roasted beetroot & rocket salad with toasted pine nuts & goat's milk cheese

This salad is such a classic combo, and one of my favourite blog recipes from 2012. Simple, elegant and earthy, it can be a starter, a side dish or a vegetarian main course. Beets are inexpensive, leaving more budget for the luxurious items like goat's milk cheese and pine nuts (these days, pine nuts are also available in smaller quantities like 40 g packets, making them much more accessible). A drizzle of balsamic vinegar rounds it off perfectly.

Serves 4

roughly 8 medium-size beetroots (or 15 small beetroots)
4 sprigs fresh thyme
80 ml (⅓ cup) extra virgin olive oil
45 ml (3 tablespoons) balsamic vinegar
juice and finely grated rind of 1 medium-size lemon
salt and freshly ground black pepper
125 ml (½ cup) water
a bunch rocket, baby spinach or watercress leaves
100 g soft goat's milk cheese (I used a log of Fairview Chevin)
about 30 ml (2 tablespoons) pine nuts, roasted in a dry pan until golden

Preheat the oven to 220 °C.

Rinse the beetroots and cut off the ends. Cut in half, or leave whole if they are small.

Arrange the beetroots in a deep roasting tray, then sprinkle with thyme leaves, olive oil, balsamic vinegar, lemon juice and rind. Season well with salt and pepper. Stir with a spatula to coat all over, then roast for 30 minutes. Remove from the oven, add the water and cover with foil. Turn down the heat to 180 °C and roast for a further 20–30 minutes until the beetroots are tender (test with a small, sharp knife). Remove from the oven, peel when cool enough to handle and then cool completely in the tray. Do not discard the tray juices.

In a large salad bowl, arrange the green leaves (I like to dress the leaves in a little olive oil and lemon juice with a pinch of salt and pepper). Slice the beetroots into smaller wedges if necessary, then coat in their juices before arranging on the leaves. Top with crumbled goat's milk cheese and roasted nuts. Serve at room temperature with extra olive oil and balsamic vinegar on the side.

roasted butternut & red onion with za'atar & tahini sauce

I'm a huge fan of Yotam Ottolenghi's superb Middle Eastern/Mediterranean recipes – if you have not heard of him, now is a good time to look him up.

We recently visited my sister at her farmhouse on Lourensford and I pledged to bring a side dish to go with their fragrant lamb curry. Seeing that I had a butternut and some tahini in my pantry, I made a version of Yotam's recipe that got rave reviews. The magic lies in the tahini dressing (another reason to make your own batch) and a little goes a long way.

I treasure recipes where humble ingredients like butternut and onions become stars, crowned with a few simple food 'jewels' like za'atar spice and parsley. This is superb served at room temperature – Mediterranean-style food fit for a king.

Serves 4

1 large butternut (about 1 kg), peeled and sliced 1 cm thick, seeds discarded
2 medium-size red onions, peeled and quartered
45 ml (3 tablespoons) extra virgin olive oil
salt and freshly ground black pepper
15-20 ml (3-4 teaspoons) Za'atar spice (page 15)
a bunch wild rocket, rinsed
80 ml (⅓ cup) whole almonds, toasted and chopped (or 30 ml/2 tablespoons roasted pine nuts)
a handful fresh parsley or coriander leaves, roughly chopped

Tahini sauce
60 ml (¼ cup) tahini (sesame paste)
30 ml (2 tablespoons) freshly squeezed lemon juice
60 ml (¼ cup) water
1 small clove garlic, finely grated
salt and freshly ground black pepper

Preheat the oven to 220 °C.

Arrange the cut butternut and onions in a large roasting tray or baking tray, preferably in a single layer. Drizzle with oil on both sides and season with salt and pepper. Roast until tender and starting to brown, about 25 minutes. Remove from the oven, sprinkle with za'atar, then return to the oven for 5–7 minutes more, taking care not to burn the sesame seeds in the spice mix. Remove from the oven and leave to cool.

For the sauce, place the tahini, lemon juice, water and garlic in a jar and season generously. Shake well until smooth and creamy.

To serve, arrange the rocket on a serving platter, then top with the roasted vegetables, nuts, parsley/coriander and a generous drizzle of tahini sauce. Serve at room temperature.

potato salad with egg, red onion, pickles, dill & wholegrain mustard dressing

Although I love a good traditional potato and mayonnaise salad, this alternative is so much fresher and brighter, with great texture. It's a wonderful side to any braaied meat or fish and is best served at room temperature.

This is one of only a few times that I'll use hard-boiled egg instead of soft – the egg should be chopped or crumbled over the salad.

Serves 6 as a side dish

about 2 kg baby potatoes
salted water, for cooking
60 ml (¼ cup) extra virgin olive oil
45 ml (3 tablespoons) wholegrain mustard
10 ml (2 teaspoons) honey
½ clove garlic, finely grated
20 ml (4 teaspoons) freshly squeezed lemon juice
a small bunch fresh dill, half of it finely chopped
salt and freshly ground black pepper
1 small red onion, finely sliced
about 125 ml (½ cup) chopped pickled gherkins
1 hard-boiled egg, finely chopped or crumbled

Cook the potatoes on the stovetop in the salted water (enough to cover them) until just tender. Drain off the water and let cool for 10–15 minutes until you're able to touch the potatoes without burning.

While the potatoes are cooling, make the dressing. In a jar, add the olive oil, mustard, honey, garlic, lemon juice, chopped dill and some salt and pepper. Shake vigorously to mix.

Halve the potatoes and place them in a large mixing bowl. Add the onion and gherkins and pour over the dressing. Toss carefully to mix, without breaking up the potatoes. Transfer to a salad bowl and top with the egg and some whole sprigs of dill.

warm chickpea salad
with cumin, olives, mint & feta

Canned chickpeas are relatively inexpensive and can be added to so many salads or stews for a nutty protein-rich kick. This warm vegetarian salad makes a great side dish to grilled lamb, or can be served as part of a tapas spread. It also makes a delightful vegetarian lunch the next day.

Serves 6

3 cans (400 g each) chickpeas, drained and rinsed
60 ml (¼ cup) extra virgin olive oil
15 ml (1 tablespoon) cumin seeds
10 ml (2 teaspoons) dried origanum
2 cloves garlic, finely grated
salt and freshly ground black pepper
30 ml (2 tablespoons) red wine vinegar
125 ml (½ cup) large kalamata olives, pitted and roughly chopped
a small bunch fresh mint leaves, finely sliced
2 rounds feta cheese, crumbled

Preheat the oven to 220 °C.

In a large mixing bowl, toss the chickpeas with the olive oil, cumin seeds, origanum and garlic, then season generously with salt and pepper. When mixed, transfer to a large deep roasting tray, and roast for about 15 minutes or until slightly darker and fragrant. Remove from the oven, then drizzle with red wine vinegar and add the olives and half of the mint. Mix carefully with a spatula – don't break it up. Transfer to a serving platter or bowl, then top with feta and the rest of the mint.

Chickpeas are incredibly versatile for use in salads, dips, stews and everything in between. This popular legume is naturally very low in fat, high in protein, iron, vitamins, fibre and antioxidants, and surprisingly gluten free.

CHAPTER 6:

pasta, potatoes & rice

As mentioned in my introduction, although South Africans love pasta and consume a massive load of it, very few of us have the tools and knowledge to make it from scratch at home. Store-bought dried pasta is economical, convenient and such a staple in so many South African homes. It's easy to whip up a sauce or add a few basic ingredients to create a fabulous meal. I have, however, included a few recipes for making your own pasta (tagliatelle and ravioli) as well as gnocchi (potato, butternut and semolina) as an ode to my favourite food group. If you do choose to make it from scratch, your efforts will be richly rewarded. Or simply replace the fresh pasta in the recipes below with your choice of store-bought for a lower effort substitute.

how to make fresh pasta

There's a firm place in my heart for store-bought dried pasta – it's one of the most convenient, comforting and cost-effective foods to cook. Dressed in a simple sauce, it becomes a quick and easy feast. But if you're willing to take the time to make pasta from scratch, few dishes can be more satisfying. Here's how to make fresh pasta from scratch. You can mix the dough by hand, but it is much quicker in a food processor. You can also roll out the dough by hand using a rolling pin, but a manual or electric pasta machine will make the job much lighter.

Serves 4

400 g cake flour, plus more for dusting
4 extra-large eggs

If making by hand
Place the flour in a large mixing bowl and make a hollow in the centre. Crack the eggs into the hollow, then use a fork to slowly whisk and mix the eggs until you have a lumpy dough. Knead the dough with your hands on a floured surface until smooth and elastic, then cover with plastic wrap and let it rest in a cool place for about 30 minutes.

If using a food processor
Place the flour and eggs in the bowl of the food processor fitted with the blade, then process until the mixture resembles coarse grains – it shouldn't come together in a ball yet (like pastry). Turn out onto a floured surface, and press the mixture together into a ball. Cover with plastic wrap and let it rest in a cool place for 30 minutes.

To roll out
Divide the dough into six pieces. Working with one piece at a time, start on the thickest/widest setting of your pasta machine and feed the dough through. Fold the sides to the centre and feed through again, then repeat for a third time. If at any time the dough looks sticky, lightly dust it with flour and continue.

Now set the pasta machine to the next (thinner) setting and feed the dough through, guiding it with your hands and taking care not to stretch it. Continue setting the machine thinner and feeding the dough through once on each setting until it is the required thickness. If using the sheets for lasagne or filled pasta like ravioli, cut it to size or fill and assemble, and use immediately. If making linguini, fettuccini or tagliatelle, attach the cutter and feed the dough through. At this point, you can hang up the pasta to dry out, or cook it immediately. If the pasta needs to stand for a while before cooking, toss it lightly in flour and leave it in coiled heaps (otherwise it will stick together).

To cook
Bring a large pot of salted water to a boil (about 15 ml/ 1 tablespoon salt per 2 litres/8 cups water). Add the pasta and cook fresh soft pasta for 2 minutes, or dried pasta for 4–6 minutes, depending on the thickness. Pasta should be cooked al dente, i.e. it still retains some firmness. (Note: Fresh cooked pasta will not have the same al dente quality as dry cooked pasta – it is inherently more tender.)

Drain the pasta (reserve some of the pasta water for thinning any sauces, if necessary) and serve immediately, drizzled with olive oil or tossed in pesto. If serving with sauce, drain and immediately add the pasta to a hot pan with just enough sauce to cover the strands. Toss to coat over medium heat for 30 seconds. Remove from the heat and plate immediately. Drizzle with extra virgin olive oil.

tagliatelle with fresh basil pesto & olive oil

This is one of the simplest yet most satisfying pasta dishes out there. We eat it weekly, sometimes making it from dried, store-bought pasta, and other times from freshly rolled and cut pasta.

Serves 4

1 batch Basil Pesto (page 47)
1 batch Fresh Pasta (page 133)
extra virgin olive oil, for drizzling
shaved pecorino or Parmesan cheese, to top
15–30 ml (1–2 tablespoons) pine nuts, roasted, to top

Prepare the basil pesto first. When done, set it aside, covering it with a thin layer of extra virgin olive oil to prevent browning.

Place a large pot of salted water over high heat. Prepare the pasta dough and feed it through the tagliatelle cutter. When the water is boiling, add the pasta and stir it carefully to loosen any sticking strands. Cook for 2–4 minutes and then drain, reserving a few tablespoons of the pasta water. Transfer the pasta to a large bowl, then top with the pesto and some extra virgin olive oil. Toss to coat, adding some of the reserved pasta water if necessary. Use tongs to plate in bowls, then top with cheese shavings and roasted pine nuts. Serve at once, with more olive oil on the side.

If you are using store-bought dry pasta for this recipe, follow the instructions for cooking on the packet – it usually takes 7–9 minutes for the perfect *al dente* result. Drain, then stir through the pesto, top with a drizzle of olive oil and a scattering of cheese and pine nuts. Serve immediately.

butternut & three-cheese ravioli with brown butter & crispy sage

This recipe was the first filled pasta I ever made and it is still one of my favourite pasta flavour combinations. To be honest, making filled pasta like ravioli is a labour of love. It takes a few hours to prepare from scratch, but gets gobbled up in minutes. The good news is that freshly assembled ravioli freezes exceptionally well, and can be cooked from frozen in a flash. Therefore, take the time and make as many as you can, then freeze in batches for a welcome, effortless dinner.

Serves 6

Roasted butternut
500 g (about 3 cups) butternut cubes (skinless and seedless)
30 ml (2 tablespoons) extra virgin olive oil
salt and freshly ground black pepper
6 fresh sage leaves, chopped
4 sprigs fresh thyme, woody stalks removed

Filling
1 batch Roasted Butternut (see above)
about 350 g (1 cup) ricotta cheese
125 g blue cheese, crumbled

about 40 g (½ cup) grated Parmesan cheese
salt and freshly ground black pepper

Pasta
1 batch Fresh Pasta (page 133)
60 ml (¼ cup) water

Sage butter and roasted pine nuts
250 g butter
20–25 fresh sage leaves
30–45 ml (2–3 tablespoons) pine nuts

For the roasted butternut, preheat the oven to 220 °C. Arrange the butternut on a baking tray, drizzle with olive oil and season with salt and pepper. Roast for 20 minutes, then scatter over the herbs and roast for a further 10 minutes until the butternut starts to turn brown and is soft when tested with a sharp knife. Remove from the oven and set aside.

For the filling, place all the ingredients in a food processor, then process to a paste. Taste and adjust seasoning if necessary. Transfer the filling to a piping bag, then set aside until ready to use (can be made ahead and refrigerated).

Prepare the pasta sheets as described on page 133 and lay them out on a large, lightly floured surface.

To assemble the ravioli, use a pastry brush to brush half of each pasta sheet lengthways with water (this is to make sure the pasta sticks when folded over lengthways after filling it). Use the prepared piping bag to pipe drops of filling lengthways down the centre of each pasta sheet, about 5 cm apart. Now fold the pasta sheet over lengthways, gently pressing out any air bubbles that are forming (press from the fold towards the edges). When each ravioli sheet is tightly sealed, used a pastry cutter to create generous rounds of individual ravioli. Place them on a floured tray until ready to boil. (The ravioli can also be frozen at this stage.)

For the sage butter, melt the butter in a small pan over medium-high heat, and let it simmer until it starts to turn light brown and smells nutty. Drop the sage leaves into the butter and swirl the pan to cover the leaves – it will bubble and spatter. The leaves will fry quickly and become crisp in 15–20 seconds. Remove from the heat at once and set aside.

In a dry pan, roast the pine nuts until golden and set aside.

To cook the ravioli, bring a large pot of salted water to a boil. When the water is boiling rapidly, drop batches of ravioli into it, then cook for 4–5 minutes. They are ready when they float on the surface and the edges are just tender. Remove with a slotted spoon into individual serving bowls. Working quickly, drizzle each portion of cooked ravioli with sage butter and top with a few toasted pine nuts. Serve at once.

greek-style youvetsi with karoo lamb, lemon & origanum

I tasted youvetsi for the first time in 2012 at food writer and social media specialist Jane-Anne Hobbs' house, as part of the launch for her cookbook, *Scrumptious*. What a revelation! In essence, it's a roasted lamb dish made with fresh tomato, origanum and lots of lemon, with flat rice-shaped pasta (orzo) cooked in the pan juices, and grilled kefalotyri cheese added on top. It's so simple, yet one of the most incredibly satisfying dishes to eat. The mouthfeel of the lemony, meaty orzo is just phenomenal, accompanied by meltingly tender lamb shreds and the grilled salty cheese. These days I make it with mutton instead of lamb, and feta instead of kefalotyri. This dish is a crowd pleaser, every time.

Serves 6

45 ml (3 tablespoons) extra virgin olive oil
2 x 1 kg mutton shanks (or roughly 1.6 kg lean mutton chops)
salt and freshly ground black pepper
30 ml (2 tablespoons) dried origanum
juice and finely grated rind of 2 medium-size lemons
6 cloves garlic, peeled and sliced
1 kg (roughly 8 large) ripe roma tomatoes, chopped
250 ml (1 cup) dry white wine
1.25 litres (5 cups) recently boiled water
500 g orzo pasta
400 g firm feta cheese
a small bunch fresh Italian parsley, chopped

Preheat the oven to 200 °C. In a very large, wide cast-iron pot or roasting pan, heat the oil on the stovetop and fry the shanks on all sides until golden brown. Season generously with salt and pepper and scatter with origanum. Remove from the heat, then add the lemon juice and rind, garlic and tomatoes. Stir to loosen any sticky bits on the bottom, then place the pot in the oven, uncovered, and roast for 15 minutes, then turn down the heat to 150 °C and roast for another 3 hours, or until the meat is very tender and starts to fall from the bone. Remove the pot from the oven and remove the meat from the pot. Shred the meat (discarding the bones) and cover it – you'll be returning it to the pot a little later.

Place the pot on the stovetop, add the wine and water and bring to a simmer. Add the orzo and cook, stirring every now and then to prevent it sticking to the bottom of the pot, until the pasta has absorbed most of the liquid and the pasta is just tender (12–15 minutes). Remove from the heat while it is still a little runnier than a risotto, because it will continue to absorb liquid while standing. Stir in the shredded meat and taste – add more salt and pepper if necessary. Cover with a lid and, while the youvetsi is resting, quickly fry the feta rounds in a hot non-stick pan in a little olive oil until golden on one side. Add the feta (roughly crumbled) on top of the youvetsi, scatter with parsley and serve at once.

pan-fried potato gnocchi with charred cream of corn & crispy bacon

This is a recipe that was born out of a book club dinner. It was my Italian-South African interpretation of an American corn salad, or succotash. In essence, it is soft pillowy potato dumplings pan-fried in butter on a bed of charred mealie cream and topped with crispy bacon nuggets, finely sliced mange tout and diced red onion.

This recipe may look a little prep intensive, but the results are well worth it. The cream of corn, brown butter and toppings can be made ahead. Serve in smaller portions, as it is quite rich.

Serves 4 as a starter or light meal

Potato gnocchi
1 kg large floury potatoes
1 extra-large egg
250 ml (1 cup) cake flour, plus extra for dusting
5 ml (1 teaspoon) fine salt
60 g butter, for frying

Charred cream of corn (make this while the potatoes are boiling)
2 fresh mealies, kernels cut from the cobs
750 ml (3 cups) fresh cream
salt and freshly ground black pepper

To serve (get these ready before you fry the gnocchi)
125 g smoked streaky bacon, finely diced and fried until crispy
a handful mange tout, finely sliced
30 ml (2 tablespoons) very finely diced red onion
pea shoots (optional)
Brown Butter (page 100)

For the gnocchi, place the potatoes (skins still on) in a pot and cover with cold water. Place on the stovetop and bring to a boil until tender (it takes about 30 minutes – continue with the charred cream of corn in the meantime). Remove from the heat and drain. Let the potatoes cool slightly, then remove the skins. While still warm, press the potatoes through a relatively coarse sieve (or use a cheese grater to grate finely) – you're looking for potato fluff, not a dense potato purée. Place the fine potatoes in a mixing bowl and add the egg, flour and salt. Stir with a fork until roughly mixed, then knead swiftly and lightly by hand to a soft dough (just a minute or so), adding more flour if needed. Divide into eight equal pieces. On a lightly floured surface, roll out each piece into long strands of about 2 cm thick, then cut into 3–4 cm lengths. Place on a lightly floured tray. When all the gnocchi are ready, fry them in butter (in batches) in a large non-stick pan.

For the charred cream of corn, dry-fry the corn kernels in a large non-stick pan over high heat, stirring often until the corn is charred and fragrant – it takes about 15 minutes. Transfer the charred kernels to a pot (reserve a few for garnishing, if you like) and add the cream. Heat up until it just starts to boil, then remove from the heat and leave to steep for 30 minutes. Transfer to a blender and blend to a purée. Press the liquid through a not-too-fine sieve in batches, removing the solids. Taste the cream and season generously with salt and pepper, then cover with a lid and set aside.

While frying the gnocchi, heat up the corn cream. To serve, ladle warm cream into wide bowls, then top with the freshly fried gnocchi, crispy bacon, sliced mange tout and onion, and top with pea shoots and the reserved corn kernels, if using. Swirl in a spoon of brown butter, then serve at once.

butternut gnocchi
with gorgonzola cream sauce

Butternut and blue cheese have always been such a fabulous flavour combination. This simple dish is punchy in flavour, rich and very satisfying. It is best served as a starter in smaller portions, but if you like rich sauces (like me), go ahead and dish up a generous bowl.

Serves 4 generously, or 6 as a starter

Gorgonzola cream sauce
500 ml (2 cups) fresh cream
250 g Gorgonzola-style blue cheese

Butternut gnocchi
600–700 g firm young butternut, halved and seeded
400 g floury potatoes, peeled
1 extra-large egg
1½ cups (375 ml) cake flour, plus extra for dusting
5 ml (1 teaspoon) fine salt
60 g butter, for frying
125 ml (½ cup) flaked almonds, roasted (to serve, optional)

For the sauce, place the cream and cheese in a medium-size saucepan over medium heat and bring to a simmer, stirring. Remove from the heat and let it stand, giving the blue cheese time to fully immerse into the cream. The sauce might look thin at this point, but it is the perfect consistency for serving with the gnocchi.

For the gnocchi, preheat the oven to 200 °C. Place the butternut and potatoes on a roasting tray and roast for about 1 hour or until tender. Remove from the oven and leave to cool slightly. Scoop out the butternut from the skin and press it through a sieve, discarding any excess liquid. Peel the potatoes and press through a sieve (or grate finely). Place the fine butternut and potato, egg, flour and salt in a mixing bowl. Stir with a fork until roughly mixed, then knead swiftly and lightly by hand to a soft dough, adding more flour if needed (it shouldn't take more than a minute or two). Divide into eight equal pieces. On a lightly floured surface, roll out each piece into long strands of about 2 cm thick, then cut into 3–4 cm lengths. Place on a lightly floured tray. When all the gnocchi are ready, fry them in butter (in batches) in a large non-stick pan. Serve in bowls with the warm blue cheese sauce, topped with flaked almonds (optionally).

Some butternuts have a higher water content than others. You're looking for a non-watery, fluffy butternut for best results. Adding too much flour will result in stodgy gnocchi.

semolina gnocchi with wild winelands mushrooms, thyme, mature cheese & cream

In Italy, they call these delicious semolina shapes Roman gnocchi, or *gnocchi alla Romana* – circles or squares cut from a cooked slab of semolina, baked in cream and mature cheese to a fabulous custardy consistency. If you're scared to roll out potato gnocchi dough but love the idea of eating gnocchi, this will become your party trick. It's almost like a creamy 'potato gratin' or a 'paptert', but made with soft-set wheaty porridge.

During autumn, you can forage wild mushrooms with an expert at Delheim and a few other establishments. Don't try to do this without the assistance of a professional, for obvious reasons.

Note: The semolina can be prepared a day or two in advance, wrapped and stored in the fridge in the slab form or in circles. Assembling and baking should be done just before serving.

Semolina slab
45 g butter, melted
35 g (½ cup) grated pecorino, grana padano, Gruyère or Parmesan cheese
3 extra-large egg yolks
salt and freshly ground black pepper
1 litre (4 cups) milk
1 ml (¼ teaspoon) ground nutmeg
200 g (1⅔ cup) semolina flour

Sauce
60 g butter, melted, plus more for frying
125 ml (½ cup) fresh cream
80 ml (⅓ cup) grated cheese (same as above)
about 250 g wild mushrooms, broken into smaller pieces if very large
salt and freshly ground black pepper
2–3 sprigs fresh thyme, leaves only
fresh micro herbs, to serve

For the gnocchi, line a 30 x 25 x 2 cm baking tray with non-stick baking paper. In a mixing bowl, whisk the butter, cheese and egg yolks and season generously with salt and pepper. Set aside. Heat the milk in a medium-large saucepan. Add the nutmeg and season with salt and pepper. When the milk starts to boil, add the semolina while stirring. Reduce the heat to medium and continue to cook, stirring, until the mixture thickens and pulls away from the sides (it takes 5–8 minutes). Watch carefully and don't let it burn. Remove from the heat. Add the egg yolk and cheese mixture and mix until smooth, working quickly. Transfer the mixture to the baking tray, edging it into the corners and smoothing the surface to an even thickness, using a spatula dipped in cold water. Set aside to cool completely.

Preheat the oven to 180 °C and grease a 25 x 18 x 5 cm baking dish. Turn the semolina slab out of the tray onto a clean working surface and peel off the baking paper. Cut the slab into circles, using a 4-cm cookie cutter or small cup dipped in cold water – or cut it into whichever shapes you like (squares, triangles etc.). Arrange the cut shapes, slightly overlapping, in the greased casserole. Now make the sauce.

For the sauce, drizzle the butter and cream over the gnocchi. Sprinkle with cheese and bake for 25–30 minutes until golden and bubbly. While the gnocchi are baking, pan-fry the mushrooms until golden. When the gnocchi come out of the oven, top with the seasoned mushrooms and herbs and serve at once.

roasted cracked baby potatoes with garlic & rosemary

These golden nuggets are totally addictive and a fantastic side dish to a larger festive spread, especially if there's some kind of sauce or gravy involved. I originally served it as part of a summery Christmas spread with roasted whole trout, Fennel, Celery and Granny Smith Apple Salad (page 108) and a mustard yoghurt dressing. It got glowing reviews and has been a favourite since.

Serves 6

Roasted potatoes
2 kg firm baby potatoes
5 ml (1 teaspoon) salt
2 heads garlic, peeled but cloves left whole (smaller cloves are best)
250 ml (1 cup) good-quality extra virgin olive oil (or canola oil, or a mixture)
salt and freshly ground black pepper
3 sprigs fresh rosemary, woody stems discarded, finely chopped

Yoghurt mayo dip
125 ml (½ cup) plain double-cream yoghurt
125 ml (½ cup) mayonnaise
15 ml (1 tablespoon) wholegrain mustard
15 ml (1 tablespoon) honey

In a large pot, add the potatoes and cover with cold water. Add the salt, then bring to a boil on the stovetop over high heat. Cook for 12–14 minutes until just tender.

Preheat the oven to 220 °C. Drain the cooking water from the potatoes, then transfer them to a large, deep roasting tray. Use the back of a dessertspoon to crack each potato gently, applying just enough pressure to leave them intact but creating nice crevices for the oil and seasoning to be absorbed.

Add the garlic cloves, drizzle the oil all over, then season generously with salt and pepper. Roast for 15 minutes, then turn each potato with tongs, scatter with rosemary and return to the oven for another 10–15 minutes until they are golden brown on both sides (keep them in longer if needed).

While the potatoes are roasting, make the mayo dip. Place all the ingredients in a small mixing bowl and mix well. Transfer to a dipping bowl and refrigerate until needed.

Remove the potatoes from the oven, then transfer to a serving dish using a slotted spoon (discard the excess oil). Serve hot with the yoghurt mayo dip.

risotto with saffron (risotto milanese)

You'll find risotto on so many South African restaurant menus. Once you get the hang of it, you can change the flavour or add ingredients as you like and create stunning versions of your own. The most important thing to remember is that the texture should be almost runny – like lava – when you serve it. Risotto will continue to thicken on standing, so don't leave it unattended once ready. Stodgy, overcooked or dry risotto just won't do. But creamy, *al dente*, well-seasoned risotto is everybody's favourite.

Risotto Milanese is probably the most famous risotto in Italy – a very simple yet luxurious version made with exotic saffron. It's an elegant starter on its own, but also a wonderful 'bed' on which to serve pan-fried fish or even roasts. A knob of butter added at the end of the cooking process will enhance the flavour and texture – it's a must. I've sprinkled my risotto with some dried Cape blossoms for colour (a mixture of nasturtium, rose mallow and bougainvillea); they're available locally from Masterstock.

Serves 4

30 ml (2 tablespoons) butter
30 ml (2 tablespoons) olive oil
1 onion, finely chopped
1 clove garlic, finely chopped
250 g arborio rice
250 ml (1 cup) dry white wine
a pinch saffron threads
1 litre (4 cups) warm chicken stock (or vegetable stock)
extra 30 ml (2 tablespoons) butter, for finishing
about 1 cup finely grated Parmesan, pecorino or grana padano cheese
salt and freshly ground black pepper
extra grated cheese, for topping
natural edible flowers, fresh or dried, for topping (optional)

In a medium-size, heavy-bottomed saucepan over medium heat, add the butter and olive oil, then fry the onion for 5–10 minutes until soft and translucent, but not brown. Add the garlic and rice, and fry for 3–4 minutes until the rice is slightly toasted and the bottom of the pan becomes dry. Add the wine and saffron, then cook, stirring very often, until the liquid has been absorbed. Add the warm stock, one ladle at a time, and cook on medium heat (stirring very often) until the liquid is almost completely absorbed before adding more. The rice should never cook completely dry – the process takes about 20 minutes, depending on your pan and your heat, so be patient.

When the rice is almost cooked but still has a slight bite (*al dente*, like pasta), add a last ladle or two of the stock and cook for about 2 minutes – the risotto should still be a little runnier than you'd like it to be, but it will continue to thicken.

Remove from the heat, then top with the extra butter and all of the cheese and cover with a lid to rest for a minute. Remove the lid, then stir to combine everything. Season with salt and pepper and serve immediately (risotto will continue to thicken on standing, so serve it at a semi-runny consistency, close to that of lava) topped with more cheese and some edible flowers.

Save any leftovers for making Arancini (see page 80).

CHAPTER 7:

grills, roasts & braises

8-hour roast pork shoulder (with crackling) with orange, fennel & paprika

There's something magical and almost primitive about a large bone-in roast. With very little attention and some patience, it becomes a feast of note – a meltingly tender pull-apart roast that tastes as good as it looks. And the crazy good crackling? Well, everybody wants it, so here's the recipe.

Serve this shoulder to a crowd as part of a festive spread – with delicious vegetable sides or as a topping on sandwiches/buns with mayo, coleslaw, salad leaves and pickles.

Serves at least 8, but will serve a large crowd if used as a pulled pork filling

about 4 kg whole pork shoulder, bone-in
30–45 ml (2–3 tablespoons) extra virgin olive oil
10 ml (2 teaspoons) salt
5 ml (1 teaspoon) freshly ground black pepper
15 ml (1 tablespoon) ground fennel
15 ml (1 tablespoon) smoked paprika
10 ml (2 teaspoons) ground coriander
10 ml (2 teaspoons) ground cumin
finely grated rind and juice of 2 oranges
375 ml (½ bottle) dry white wine

Preheat the oven to 120 °C. Remove the skin of the shoulder using a sharp knife. Place the skin on a wire rack and refrigerate, uncovered, until later.

Place the shoulder in your largest deep roasting tray. Rub with olive oil. Mix the salt, pepper, fennel, paprika, coriander, cumin and orange rind, then rub it all over the meat. Pour the orange juice and wine into the tray, then cover with heavy-duty foil and roast for 8 hours until falling from the bone and really tender.

Serve warm, pulling the meat apart to soak in the pan juices, with sides or pasta, and a piece of crispy crackling on the side.

crackling

There are only a few key points to a successful crackling:
- Dry out the skin.
- Season generously with salt.
- Cook over high heat.

Score the skin in parallel lines using a very sharp blade or NT cutter (or ask your butcher to do it). The reserved skin layer of the pork shoulder should spend at least 8 hours in the fridge, uncovered, drying out on a wire rack.

About 1 hour before serving the meat, remove the roast from the oven (keep it covered) and turn the heat up to the highest setting (230–260 °C). Salt the dried-out skin, rubbing the salt into the scored lines. Place the salted layer of skin in the preheated oven and roast for 30–45 minutes (depending on thickness) on a setting above the middle rack, until bubbling up and very crispy and golden (don't let it get too dark). Remove and let it cool. Cut into shards and serve with the roast. (Can be prepared an hour or two in advance.)

slow-roasted leg of lamb with white wine, rosemary & garlic

This is such a simple, classic combination. I associate the smell, taste and texture of this roast with Christmas and special occasions – when you want to treat family or friends to something beautiful. It's tempting to want to change the simplicity of the ingredients, but don't. It's good enough and simply spectacular as is.

Serves 4–6

1 x 2.5 kg leg of lamb (or mutton), bone-in
salt and freshly ground black pepper
about 10 cloves garlic, peeled
about 5 sprigs fresh rosemary
30 ml (2 tablespoons) extra virgin olive oil
375 ml (½ bottle) dry white wine

Preheat the oven to 150 °C. Place the leg, fat-side up, in a large roasting tray. Season well with salt and pepper. Using a small, sharp knife, make small incisions all over the leg. Use the garlic cloves (cut large cloves in half lengthways or in quarters) and rosemary sprigs to stuff into the incisions. Drizzle all over with olive oil, then pour the wine into the bottom of the tray. Cover with foil, then roast for 4 hours or until really tender and falling from the bone. Remove the foil, turn the heat up to maximum and grill for about 10 minutes or until golden. Serve at once, or cover with foil and reheat before serving.

For a Greek-inspired twist, add about 125 ml (½ cup) freshly squeezed lemon juice before roasting. The sharp lemon flavour cuts through the fattiness of the lamb beautifully.

coq au cape riesling

There's a very traditional and popular French chicken stew called *coq au vin* or 'chicken in wine' (mostly red wine) that has been a global favourite for decades. This version uses an aromatic white wine, Riesling, to make the most of our local Mediterranean heritage – we've cooked chicken in wine for decades anyway. The Helshoogte and Elgin wine valleys produce incredible Rieslings – it's a cultivar that deserves a lot more attention and is an exceptional food pairing wine. Choose excellent quality locally farmed free-range chicken for this recipe.

Serves 4–6, but this recipe can easily be doubled to feed a large crowd

45 ml (3 tablespoons) extra virgin olive oil
8 chicken pieces (about 1 kg)
16–20 small pearl onions (also called pickling onions), skinned and whole
125 g streaky bacon, chopped
3 sprigs fresh thyme, woody stalks removed
250 g portabellini mushrooms, halved
30 ml (2 tablespoons) flour
375 ml (½ bottle) dry Riesling
salt and freshly ground black pepper
a handful fresh Italian parsley, roughly chopped, to serve
cooked rice, pasta, potatoes or bread, to serve

In a large heavy-bottomed saucepan, heat the olive oil over medium-high heat, then fry the chicken pieces in batches until the skins are golden. Remove from the pan and set aside.

Add the onions, bacon and thyme to the same pan, then fry until the bacon becomes crispy and the onions start to get some colour. Add the mushrooms and fry for another minute.

Add the flour, then stir to coat the mixture all over. Add the Riesling and stir well. Return the chicken pieces and meat juices back into the pan. Bring to a simmer, then turn the heat down to low, cover and simmer for 1 hour 15 minutes. Check on the chicken every now and then to make sure that the pieces are submerged in the sauce.

Season with salt and pepper, then stir gently without breaking up the meat. Serve warm (scattered with parsley) with rice, potatoes, pasta or bread, and some steamed green vegetables like green beans or broccolini.

pan-fried trout fillets with lemon, dill & apricot butter sauce

My brother-in-law, Gerhard Compion, is a trout farmer on Lourensford Estate in Somerset West. A few years ago, I was involved in the family business with processing and distribution, and I've had the pleasure of cooking and experimenting with fresh trout very often. It's a superb fish to eat – tender, fragrant and easy to pinbone and serve boneless.

Although I'll eat trout any possible way, this recipe remains right at the top. The marinade can also be used for grilling the fish over a fire, and works very well on other fish, such as snoek and yellowtail.

Serves 4

125 g butter
juice and finely grated rind of 1 lemon (plus more, if needed)
30 ml (2 tablespoons) smooth apricot jam
10 ml (2 teaspoons) soy sauce (optional)
1 clove garlic, finely grated
a few sprigs fresh dill, finely chopped (about 2 tablespoons)
salt and freshly ground black pepper
about 600 g trimmed pinboned trout fillets, skin on
45 ml (3 tablespoons) extra virgin olive oil

Melt the butter in a small pot, then add the lemon juice and rind, jam, soy sauce, garlic and dill and season generously with salt and pepper. Stir and bring to a simmer. Cook for 2–3 minutes, stirring, then remove from the heat and set aside. Taste and adjust seasoning if necessary.

Rinse the trout fillets under cold running water and pat dry with a clean tea towel or kitchen paper. Cut the fish into four portions and season with salt and pepper. Heat the oil in a large non-stick pan (non-stick is crucial, as the flesh-side of the fish easily sticks to regular pans). When the pan is hot, add the fillets, skin-side down, and cook for 4–5 minutes or until the edges start to turn pink and the skin is crispy. Working quickly, use a pastry brush to coat the flesh side in marinade, then turn the fish over for just a minute or so to get some colour. You're aiming for a result that is still ever-so-slightly undercooked in the centre. Remove from the pan and transfer to a serving platter, skin-side down. Brush the fish again with the butter sauce to give it a nice shine.

Serve with Fennel, Celery and Granny Smith Apple Salad (page 108) and Creamed Cauliflower with Brown Butter and Gruyère Cheese (page 100) or your choice of salad and sides.

roasted farm chicken with garlic & thyme

These days the standard supermarket chickens available in South Africa are so tiny, it's a shame. We might forget that chickens can actually be big and plump with beautiful dark meat, if they're left to roam and grow properly. A 'farm chicken' of 2–3 kg can easily feed a family of six – sometimes with leftovers.

The Boer & Butcher in Stellenbosch (also with a branch in Durbanville) stocks beautiful large farm chickens. They taste like chicken should taste, and they make a show-stopping centrepiece roast on a generous lunch or dinner table.

Take your time with roasting a whole chicken – it should easily fall from the bone and that takes a little time (although less than red meat). A heavy-bottomed pot like a flat iron pot or a Le Creuset pot delivers the best results. Simplicity is king, and the beautiful meat is the hero (aside from the crispy, golden skin, of course).

Serves 6

45 ml (3 tablespoons) extra virgin olive oil
1 large free-range farm chicken (about 2.5 kg)
2 onions, quartered
about 16 whole garlic cloves, unpeeled
6 sprigs fresh thyme
salt and freshly ground black pepper

Preheat the oven to 180 °C. Drizzle the bottom of a very large heavy-bottomed pot (like a 30 cm Le Creuset casserole) with some of the olive oil. Place the chicken in the pot, breast-side up. Drizzle with more oil and rub all over the chicken. Arrange the onions and garlic around the chicken and top with thyme. Season generously all over with salt and pepper. Roast for 2 hours until golden brown and very tender. Serve warm with Roasted Cracked Baby Potatoes with Garlic and Rosemary (page 146) and a Green on Green Salad (page 112).

Don't fuss too much about how to carve a roast chicken. The chicken should be tender enough to gently pull apart with tongs. The large breasts can be sliced into smaller chunks. Make sure everyone gets a piece of crispy skin.

braaied stuffed whole fish with lemon, feta & herbs

Cape yellowtail (*geelstert*) or cob are both green listed on SASSI and some of my favourite fish to cook. A smaller fish is perfect for a midweek dinner and can easily be cooked in the oven, seasoned with salt and pepper and served with garlic-butter or a squeeze of lemon. Over weekends, cooking it over a fire is the best – the flavour of fire-roasted fish in the air smells like holiday and good times.

A gutted whole fish simply asks for a generous stuffing. I've used thinly sliced lemon, feta, herbs and butter, but you can also use sliced onion or tomatoes. Serve the fish on a platter, whole, topped with more fresh herbs and perhaps some grilled vegetables and a Roasted Garlic Butter Loaf (page 33).

Serves 4

1 fresh whole yellowtail, gutted (about 1.5 kg)
45 ml (3 tablespoons) butter, melted
salt and freshly ground black pepper
1 small lemon, very thinly sliced (a mandoline works best)
2 rounds feta, sliced into thinner rounds horizontally
a small bunch fresh parsley, chopped

Rinse the fish under running water and pat dry completely with kitchen paper or a clean cloth. Drizzle the cavity generously with the melted butter, then season with salt and pepper. Insert the sliced lemon (overlapping) and rounds of feta, then scatter with parsley and close the fish neatly with a few toothpicks or a skewer. Braai over medium-hot coals, turning often – for about 20 minutes or until cooked right through to the centre and golden on the outside. Serve as suggested above.

Most fresh whole fish can be cooked in this way. Choose sustainably caught fish that is green listed – if in doubt, check online at wwfsassi.co.za/sassi-list/.

pork & fennel ragu
with tomato & preserved lemon

This 'white bolognese' pork ragu is a superb alternative to the much-loved and better-known beef ragu. Made with pork mince, white wine, fennel seeds, smoked paprika, fresh tomatoes and zesty preserved lemon, it has a fragrance that is unusual and inviting. Using fresh tomatoes (and no tomato paste) results in a lighter end result than using canned tomatoes, with a less intense tomato flavour.

Serves 6

60 ml (¼ cup) extra virgin olive oil, plus extra for drizzling
1 onion, chopped
1 small fennel bulb, finely chopped (1–2 cups)
1 carrot, peeled and finely chopped
4 cloves garlic, finely chopped
6 sprigs fresh thyme, woody stalks removed
10 sage leaves, finely chopped
15 ml (1 tablespoon) fennel seeds
15 ml (1 tablespoon) smoked paprika
1 kg quality pork mince (coarsely minced, if possible)
250 ml (1 cup) dry white wine
6 ripe tomatoes, processed to a pulp
salt and freshly ground black pepper
125 ml (½ cup) fresh cream (optional)
about 15 ml (1 tablespoon) finely chopped Preserved Lemon rind (page 184, or use freshly grated lemon rind),
    plus more to serve
shaved semi-hard goat's milk cheese, to serve (optional)
a handful fresh Italian parsley, roughly chopped, to serve (optional)

Heat the oil in a large (5–6 litre capacity) heavy-bottomed pot (with lid) over medium heat. Add the onion, fennel and carrot and fry until soft (don't rush it). Add the garlic, thyme, sage, fennel seeds and paprika and fry for another few minutes until the bottom of the pot starts to go brown, but not too dark. Add the mince and stir to break up any lumps. Turn the heat up to high and fry until the meat is brown all over and the meaty juices have evaporated (it will take 10–15 minutes). Continue to fry, stirring, until the meat releases its own fat and starts to catch on the bottom – this step is crucial for building deeper flavour. Add the wine and stir to loosen any sticky bits on the bottom. Add the tomatoes, season with salt and pepper and bring to a simmer. Turn the heat down to low, cover with the lid and cook for 2 hours, stirring every now and then to prevent the bottom from burning. Remove from the heat, add the cream and lemon rind and stir. Taste and add more salt and pepper if necessary.

Serve hot in bowls with pasta or gnocchi, with shaved goat's milk cheese and scattered parsley and a drizzle of extra virgin olive oil.

CHAPTER 8:

desserts

I've only included a few of my all-time favourites here, because if left to my own devices I'll probably write a whole new book on cakes, tarts, pastries and sweets alone. The following collection of (mostly fruit-driven) desserts are the ones that I serve often when I entertain friends and family – they're all trusted crowd-pleasers.

cape stone fruit galette

I've made so many different versions of this free-form tart, my favourites being with sliced stone fruit such as peaches, or with blueberries. In essence, it is a fantastic combination of buttery, flaky pastry topped with grated or shaved almond paste and soft sliced fruit. The almond is essential, as it gives a lot of sweetness and gooey texture in the middle that contrasts well with the flaky pastry and tart fruit. This dessert can be made ahead and reheated in the oven, and served with vanilla ice cream.

Note: You can substitute the almond paste with store-bought marzipan or even persipan (the more economical marzipan substitute made with apricot kernels – great for baking). The recipe makes two galettes – although one galette can serve six people, everybody asks for seconds, so it's good to have a backup. Any leftovers will be gobbled up for breakfast at our house.

Serves 6

Almond paste (make this ahead as it needs to firm up in the freezer for at least 1 hour)
100 g (1 cup) whole blanched almonds
250 ml (1 cup) icing sugar
1 ml (¼ teaspoon) almond essence
1 extra-large egg white, whisked with a fork to break up the texture (you only need half; keep the rest for later)

Pastry
280 g (2 cups) cake flour
60 ml (¼ cup) castor sugar
5 ml (½ teaspoon) salt
250 g cold butter, diced
60 ml (¼ cup) ice water

Topping (enough for 2 galettes)
1 batch Almond Paste (see above)
6 large stone fruits of choice, peeled and sliced (pips removed)
15–30 ml (1–2 tablespoons) cinnamon sugar

For the almond paste, place the almonds in a food processor and process until very fine. Add the icing sugar, almond essence and about 15 ml (1 tablespoon) of the egg white. Process until it forms a sticky ball (add a little more egg white until it just comes together, or add a little more icing sugar if it is too wet). Remove and transfer to a sheet of plastic wrap. Cover the ball with the plastic and freeze until firm.

For the pastry, place the flour, castor sugar, salt and butter in a food processor. Pulse until it resembles coarse crumbs. Add the cold water and process until it just starts to come together in a ball. Remove from the bowl and press together, then wrap in plastic wrap and refrigerate for 30 minutes.

Preheat the oven to 220 °C. Roll out the pastry in a circular shape on a lightly floured surface to a thickness of about 5 mm. Transfer carefully to a large baking tray lined with non-stick baking paper. Brush the surface of the pastry with the leftover egg white, leaving a 3-cm border. Coarsely grate the almond paste in an even layer over the brushed pastry surface, then arrange the sliced fruit on top. Fold over the edges to create a foldover edge of about 3 cm, then sprinkle with cinnamon sugar. Bake for 25–30 minutes until golden brown. Remove from the oven, slice and serve hot with vanilla ice cream (can also be eaten at room temperature).

pavlova with lemon curd & passion fruit

I cannot count the number of pavlovas I've made in my life, but it must be close to 100. It's just such a stunning way to end a festive lunch or dinner and the toppings can be changed seasonally. The easiest way to serve it is with seasonal fruit and whipped cream. But since you're using six egg whites for the meringue, you might as well make a silky lemon curd with the yolks. With added fresh passion fruit, this is the stuff summer dreams are made of.

Serves 8

6 extra-large egg whites (save the yolks and make lemon curd*)
400 g castor sugar
10 ml (2 teaspoons) white vinegar or lemon juice
15 ml (1 tablespoon) cornflour
5 ml (1 teaspoon) vanilla extract (or scraped seeds of 1 vanilla pod)
250 ml (1 cup) fresh cream, whipped
about 250 ml (1 cup) lemon curd, for topping (page 188)*
pulp of about 4 fresh passion fruits (granadillas)

Preheat the oven to 150 °C.

Whisk the egg whites in a large bowl (with an electric whisk or stand mixer with whisk attachment) until soft peaks form. Gradually add the castor sugar to the egg whites, small amounts at a time, whisking constantly until the mixture is stiff and glossy. Add the vinegar or lemon juice, cornflour and vanilla and mix well.

Dot a large roasting tray with some of the mixture, then place a sheet of baking paper on top (so that it sticks like glue). Pour the pavlova mixture onto the tray and shape with a spoon or spatula into a circle with a diameter of about 23 cm (draw a circle on the back of your baking paper, if necessary). The mixture will rise a bit around the sides, so leave enough space. Place in the oven and immediately turn down the temperature to 120 °C. Bake for 1¼ hours, then switch the oven off and leave to cool in the oven for about 2½ hours without opening the oven door.

To serve: Carefully remove the baking paper from the bottom of the pavlova and transfer to a serving dish (it will have a few cracks, but that's 100%). Top with whipped cream and lemon curd, swirling the cream and curd together softly. Top with lashings of passion fruit pulp and serve at once, sliced.

Pavlova must be assembled just before serving as it becomes soggy on standing. Store the unassembled baked meringue on the baking tray covered with a sealed large plastic bag. It can be baked a day ahead if stored in an airtight container.

white tiramisu with brandy

You'll find tiramisu on many restaurant menus in South Africa, and in many South African-authored cookbooks. I see it as part of our fridge tart fixation – just think Peppermint Crisp tart, cottage cheese tart and Cremora tart, to name a few.

Tiramisu means 'pick me up' or 'cheer me up' in Italian, mainly because of the coffee kick. Many different liquors are used all over the world, but for me a South African brandy works best. I add a little more than most recipes, because I love the flavour combination of coffee and brandy very much and feel that they should be equally strong. Keep in mind then that this is obviously not suitable for the young ones, so keep some ice cream and a few sugar cones handy when entertaining families with kids.

Note: This dessert needs time in the fridge to develop in flavour and for the biscuits to fully soften. It is best made a day or two ahead, kept refrigerated.

Serves 6

5 extra-large eggs, separated (keep 3 egg whites separate from the other 2)
260 g (1¼ cups) castor sugar
2 tubs (250 g each) mascarpone cheese, at room temperature
375 ml (1½ cups) strong black coffee, slightly cooled
80 ml (⅓ cup) brandy
1 packet (200 g) 'sponge fingers' (finger biscuits)
shaved white chocolate and roasted flaked almonds, to serve (optional)

Separate the eggs into two mixing bowls, one for yolks and one for whites. Using electric beaters, whisk the egg yolks with the castor sugar on high speed until the mixture turns a pale yellow colour and doubles in volume (4–5 minutes). Add the mascarpone and whisk until the mixture is smooth (about 30 seconds).

Rinse the whisk/beaters and dry thoroughly. In the other mixing bowl, use the clean beaters to whisk 3 of the egg whites until they are thick and hold their shape (stiff peak stage). Using a large spoon, add the whisked egg whites in 2–3 batches to the mascarpone mixture, folding it in lightly until smooth. Set aside.

Mix the coffee and brandy in a separate wide bowl, wide enough to fit the length of the biscuits when dipped. Dip one biscuit at a time into the mixture (don't soak them too long, just dip them swiftly) and arrange them in a single layer with no gaps in a medium-size deep rectangular or square dish – half of the biscuits should cover the full surface area of the dish. Cover the soaked biscuit layer with half of the mascarpone mixture, spreading it evenly into the corners. Then repeat with another layer of dipped biscuits. Top with the remaining half of the mascarpone mixture, smoothing the top (or transfer it to a piping bag and pipe neat rows for a spectacular look). Cover with plastic wrap (the dish should be deep enough that the plastic won't touch the top of the tiramisu or it will spoil the beautiful surface) and refrigerate for at least 3 hours or preferably overnight.

Top with shaved white chocolate and roasted almond flakes just before serving. Cut into squares and serve cold.

baked cape figs with fynbos honey & gorgonzola

There are a few exceptional Gorgonzola-style blue cheeses made in South Africa. One is from Cremona – so silky and creamy that it literally melts in your mouth. Only choose a really good-quality cheese when serving this simple yet elegant dessert. The combination of the salty, rich cheese and the warm baked figs is, quite literally, heaven on a plate.

Serves 4

12 ripe black figs
30 ml (2 tablespoons) fynbos honey, to drizzle
about 250 g Gorgonzola-style blue cheese
melba toast or crackers, to serve (optional)

Preheat the oven to 180 °C. Cut off the hard tops of the figs and make a cross incision at the top of each fig. Arrange the figs on a small baking tray, standing up (level out their bottoms with a sharp knife, if necessary). Drizzle with honey, then bake for 10 minutes until tender but still intact. Serve hot with the cheese and perhaps some melba toast or crackers.

At the time of shooting the photographs for this book, figs were out of season. In the Western Cape, locally farmed purple figs are far superior for this recipe than their greener imported cousins. Look out for these local purple beauties from mid-summer to late autumn.

vanilla meringues with berry sauce & cream

A generous bowl full of voluptuous homemade meringues always gets oohs and ahs, their swirly shapes just mesmerising. It's amazing what you can do with a few egg whites and some sugar – it's one of those 'alchemy' moments to see the gloopy liquid transform into silky, glossy, pure white tufts.

Keep a few berries whole to serve, and cook the rest down to a chunky, sweet and tart sauce. Create a self-help 'Eaton mess' station – your guests will be more than happy to dish up their own – it's part of the fun!

Serves 6

Meringues
4 egg whites
a pinch salt
210 g (1 cup) castor sugar
seeds of 1 vanilla pod (or 5 ml/1 teaspoon vanilla extract)

Berry sauce
400–500 g fresh mixed berries
juice of 1 lemon
105 g (½ cup) castor sugar

To serve
1 batch Meringues (see above)
1 batch Berry Sauce (see above)
250 ml (1 cup) fresh cream, whipped to soft peaks

For the meringues, preheat the oven to 100 °C. Whisk the egg whites and salt on full speed in a large mixing bowl. When the whites begin to form soft peaks, add the sugar, little by little, whisking continuously. When all the sugar is incorporated, add the vanilla and mix well. On a large baking tray (you might need more than one) lined with non-stick baking paper, drop spoonsful of meringue mixture about the size of a golf ball (use two spoons, one to scoop and the other to release the mixture), making sure to leave dramatic swirls on top. Bake for 1 hour, then remove from the oven and cool completely.

For the sauce, place most of the berries (reserve a few for serving whole), lemon juice and castor sugar in a small pot over medium heat. Stir every now and then until the fruit starts to break up and become soft. Simmer for 5 minutes over low heat, breaking it up further with a fork or spoon. Remove from the heat and cool.

Serve in tall glasses, creating layers of meringues, berry sauce, whole berries and cream, or in bowls.

honey, rose-water & cinnamon panna cotta

Panna cottas are a fabulous make-ahead dessert if you're planning a feast and want to save yourself some effort on game day. The silky, cool texture is so pleasing on a hot summer's day. This version takes on some beautifully perfumed Turkish delight flavours. However, if rose-water is not your thing, just leave it out.

Turn your panna cottas out by carefully dipping the moulds into hot water for a few seconds, then turn over onto a plate and give it a firm shake. However, if you don't want the stress of turning out the panna cottas right before serving, just set the mixture in beautiful glasses and serve as is.

Serves 4

500 ml (2 cups) fresh cream
10 ml (2 teaspoons) powdered gelatine
60 ml (¼ cup) sugar
20 ml (4 teaspoons) honey, plus more for serving
1 cinnamon stick
10 ml (2 teaspoons) rose-water
honey, to drizzle
sliced fresh strawberries, to serve (optional)

Lightly spray four small ramekins (160–180 ml capacity) with non-stick cooking spray and set aside.

Pour 45 ml (3 tablespoons) of the cream into a cup and mix with the gelatine. Leave the mixture for 10 minutes to sponge.

In the meantime, heat the rest of the cream, sugar, honey, cinnamon stick and rose-water in a small pot on the stove, stirring, until the sugar has melted (do not boil). Add the sponged gelatine mixture and stir gently to melt. Remove from the heat, remove the cinnamon stick and pour into four ramekins or glasses. Cool and refrigerate until set (about 1 hour). Serve with a drizzle of honey and (optionally) sliced fresh strawberries.

The drizzle of honey on the top of the panna cottas takes a few minutes to 'melt' and spread into a smooth, thin layer. Tilt the ramekins from side to side to help it spread.

baklava cigars
with citrus & spices

My friend, Maaika Kruger, lives in Turkey and recently brought me a tub full of Turkish pastries. And do those Turks know their sweets! They were some of the best little sweet treats I've ever had, most of them nut-based and made with flaky filo pastry. These luxurious filo rolls are filled with a mixed nut and citrus paste and were inspired by the sweet Turkish treasure trove from Maaika – they are such a stunning end to a Mediterranean lunch or dinner, served with coffee or a good brandy. They also make a good addition to a tea table spread.

Makes 18

Syrup
400 g (2 cups) white sugar
500 ml (2 cups) water
30 ml (2 tablespoons) honey
2 whole cloves
peeled rind of ½ lemon

For the syrup, bring all the ingredients to a boil in a small pot, then cook rapidly for 5 minutes. Remove from the heat and set aside.

Filo cigars
100 g raw almonds
100 g walnuts
finely grated rind of 1 lemon
finely grated rind of 1 orange
5 ml (1 teaspoon) ground cinnamon
60 ml (¼ cup) icing sugar
1 ml (¼ teaspoon) salt
1 extra-large egg white
2.5 ml (½ teaspoon) almond essence
6 sheets filo pastry
about 80 ml (⅓ cup) canola oil
30 ml (2 tablespoons) shelled whole pistachios, finely chopped (optional)

For the filo cigars, place the almonds and walnuts in a food processor and process until finely chopped (don't take it too far, you don't want to make a nut butter). Add the grated citrus rind, cinnamon, icing sugar, salt and egg white and process to a paste. Divide into six parts and roll out into long snakes of about 1.5 cm thickness and 21 cm length.

Preheat the oven to 200 °C. Working with one sheet of filo (21 x 34 cm) at a time on a large working surface, brush with oil all over, then place a rolled-out nut shape on one end. Roll it up neatly, then cut each into equal parts of about 7 cm each. Arrange tightly in a baking tray sprayed with non-stick spray and bake for 18–20 minutes or until golden brown. While the cigars are baking, gently reheat the syrup. Remove the cigars from the oven and pour the hot syrup over them. Leave to cool in the tray. When cool, remove from the syrup, scatter with some finely chopped pistachios and serve.

CHAPTER 9:

preserves

preserved lemons

Preserved lemons are not readily available in supermarkets in South Africa, so it's a wise decision to make your own. They're ready to use after one month but, in my opinion, they are better from three months onwards. Once opened, they can be kept in the refrigerator almost indefinitely – they will darken with age (I've had some that were two years old and they were still fantastic) and eventually fall apart, but they're still good to use. Preferably you'll use them often enough to never have to keep them for longer than a year.

Lemons are preserved in salt (not sugar), and you'll only use the rind (the flesh is discarded), sliced or chopped. Use sparingly – it adds intense lemon flavour to stews and other meat dishes and is a wonderful, exotic addition to your Cape Mediterranean pantry.

Makes 1 x 1-litre jar

about 7 small or medium-size organic lemons (make sure they are not waxed)
about 100 g coarse salt
1 bay leaf
10 black peppercorns
1 stick cinnamon
250–350 ml boiled water, cooled

Sterilise a 1-litre capacity wide-mouthed jar and leave it to cool. Cut a deep cross into the top of five of the lemons (about three-quarter way through, with the bases still joined) – you'll use the remaining two for juice only. Use a teaspoon to pack about 10 ml (2 teaspoons) of salt into the cut section of one lemon, then place it inside the jar. Cover with 5 ml (1 teaspoon) salt, then repeat with more salted lemons until the jar is full. Pack the lemons as tightly as possible. Add the bay leaf, peppercorns and cinnamon stick halfway through. Squeeze the juice of the remaining two lemons, then add it to the jar. Top up with cooled boiled water, then seal tightly.

Store in a cool, dark place, and gently shake the jar every few days for the first week or two to make sure the salt dissolves fully. The lemons will be ready for use within one month, but will develop in intensity with age. Once opened, refrigerate immediately.

spiced citrus marmalade

Every winter, with the appearance of the first seasonal oranges, I buy a large bag and make marmalade. It lasts us all year long and makes for great little gifts along the way. Marmalade on toast (especially on mosbolletjie toast) must be one of the most comforting breakfasts out there. If you're not already a fan, try it soon. The addition of spices makes the marmalade taste wonderfully perfumed and layered in flavour.

Makes about 1 litre

1 kg oranges
grated rind and juice of 1 lemon
750 ml (3 cups) water
1 kg white sugar
1 whole clove
1 star anise
1 stick cinnamon
2 cardamom pods

Using a mandoline cutter or very sharp knife, slice the oranges thinly, discarding the ends. Add the sliced oranges, lemon rind and juice and water to a medium-size stockpot (or jam pot), then heat to boiling point. Reduce to a slow simmer, then cook for 40 minutes until soft.

Add the sugar and spices, then cook for another 30–60 minutes (depending on the size of the pot and the temperature) until soft setting point (skim off any scum forming on the top layer). For soft setting point, test a teaspoon of the boiling liquid on a cooled saucer – it should have a soft-set gel-like texture. Don't let the mixture get too dark.

When the desired texture is reached, transfer the marmalade to sterilised glass jars, then seal immediately. Store on a cool shelf and refrigerate after opening (it will last in the fridge for many weeks). Serve on buttered toast or as part of a bread and cheese spread (the marmalade is also very good served with soft cheeses such as Brie and Camembert).

This recipe can easily be doubled of tripled according to your available produce. Always use a bigger pot than you think you'll need – jams need space to release moisture and become syrupy before setting.

lemon curd

You only need three lemons to make 500 ml (2 cups) lemon curd. It's a phenomenal spread for cakes, cookies or even a pavlova, and will last for at least a week in the refrigerator, once opened. I must confess, I sometimes eat it straight from the jar with a spoon, because it is so delicious..

I usually make my lemon curd with four whole eggs, but when I've made a pavlova using six egg whites, I use the remaining six yolks instead of whole eggs. Use whatever you have on hand.

Makes 500 ml (2 cups)

peeled rind and juice of 3 medium-size lemons
250 ml (1 cup) white sugar
180 g soft butter
4 extra-large eggs (or 6 extra-large egg yolks)
a pinch salt

Place the peeled rind and sugar in a food processor and process until you get a very fine, yellow, grainy mixture. Add the butter and process until light and creamy. Add the eggs and salt and mix well, scraping the sides of the bowl. Add the lemon juice and mix until smooth. Transfer to a small saucepan over very low heat. Stir continuously while it heats up (take care, it burns easily). The mixture will at first become runnier as the butter starts to melt, and then it will thicken again as the eggs form a glossy custard. Never let it reach boiling point. If at any stage it looks like it's burning, remove from the heat at once and strain to remove any brown bits. Remove from the heat and transfer to a glass jar with a lid. Cool and refrigerate until ready to use. (Note: For an ultra-silky result, strain the hot mixture before cooling.)

Best served at room temperature – spread it on cakes or cookies, or serve with meringues (Eaton mess-style) and on pavlova (with whipped cream and toasted almonds).

If you're using six egg yolks to make this curd, you can use the whites to make a fabulous pavlova (page 170). A curd made with yolks tends to burn a little more easily than one made with whole eggs, so cook it over low heat and watch it carefully – it's definitely worth it!

port-soaked cranberries

These delightful halfmoon rubies don't take long to make and they are so versatile. They last wonderfully long in the fridge (at least a month) because they're made with dried preserved cranberries to begin with. Serve with a cheese board, with a meaty terrine, with cold cuts or even with a delicious festive roast.

Makes about 375 ml (1½ cups)

100 g (1 cup) dried cranberries
½ cup (125 ml) port wine
1 star anise, 1 whole clove, 1 cinnamon stick (optional)

Place cranberries and port (and spices, if using) in a small pot, then heat to a simmer. Cook over low heat for about 10 minutes or until most of the port is absorbed, stirring occasionally (don't let it cook dry). Remove from the heat, transfer to a glass container and set aside to cool. Store in the refrigerator, covered. Serve at room temperature.

See page 73 for photograph.

RECIPE INDEX

THANK YOU

Thank you to my best friend and husband, Schalk, for encouraging me to follow my heart, even at the early stages of my blog when we had no money but still somehow managed to not only have food on the table, but eat like kings. This book is dedicated to you, my love.

To my dearest friend and photographer/stylist partner in creating this book, Tasha Seccombe – thank you for being a force of incredible inspiration, creativity, talent and stamina in taking on this project with me. Thank you for your patience and insight, and for letting me use your brand-new home and your brand-spanking-new stove for the shoot. I wouldn't have done this with anyone else but you by my side.

This is my first book and I couldn't have asked for a more well-oiled support system to make it happen. Thank you to Linda de Villiers, Helen Henn, Joy Clack and the friendly, professional team from Penguin Random House for giving my ideas a platform in print. It's been a dream of mine for so many years, and you made it a reality.

Thank you to the team of Mervyn Gers Ceramics who generously loaned so many of their ceramics to us for this project. You made my vision of 'teal, blue, green and everything in between' come to life.

Thank you also to my good friend Katrin Hermann van Dyk of Hertex and Hertex HAUS for providing us with the most beautiful textiles, wall papers, cutlery and selection of ceramics to use for the shoot. We couldn't have asked for a more beautiful collection of textures and colours.

Thank you to Southern Art Ceramics for the stunning original Delft-style painted tiles and rustic teal rectangular tiles that served as backgrounds in many of the photographs.

Thank you to my sister, Erna Compion, and her husband, Gerhard, for letting us use their home for the al fresco shoot and the front cover. And thank you, Gerhard, for the fantastic trout that we photographed that day – such a privilege to be able to get such fresh fish directly from the farmer.

Thank you to Nooitgedacht outside Stellenbosch for allowing us to take photographs at their stunning blue-tiled wall.

Thank you to Boschendal at Oude Bank for allowing us to take photographs at their beautiful shop.

And thank you to Marius and the friendly team from Bergzicht Furniture for the use of that magnificent fridge for the duration of the shoot.